INTERNATIONAL DEVELOPMENT IN FOCUS

Health Financing Reform in Ukraine

Progress and Future Directions

CARYN BREDENKAMP, ELINA DALE, OLENA DOROSHENKO, YURIY DZHYGYR,
JARNO HABICHT, LORAINE HAWKINS, ALEXANDR KATSAGA,
KATERYNA MAYNZYUK, KHRYSTYNA PAK, AND OLGA ZUES

Contents

Figures

Tables

Acknowledgments

This report on Ukraine health financing reform was prepared by the World Bank and the World Health Organization (WHO) Regional Office for Europe. The authors of the report are, in alphabetical order, Caryn Bredenkamp (World Bank), Elina Dale (WHO Country Office in Ukraine), Olena Doroshenko (World Bank), Yuriy Dzhygyr (World Bank consultant), Jarno Habicht (WHO Country Office in Ukraine), Loraine Hawkins (independent consultant), Alexandr Katsaga (independent consultant), Kateryna Maynzyuk (World Bank consultant), Khrystyna Pak (World Bank consultant), and Olga Zeus (independent consultant).

The report also benefited from comments and inputs received from Paolo Belli (World Bank), Tania Dmytraczenko (World Bank), Tamás Evetovits (WHO Barcelona Office for Health Systems Financing), Triin Habicht (WHO Barcelona Office for Health Systems Financing), Tehmina Khan (World Bank), Toomas Palu (World Bank), Tomáš Roubal (WHO Country Office in Ukraine), Karlis Smits (World Bank), and Sarah Thomson (WHO Barcelona Office for Health Systems Financing).

The World Bank and the WHO Regional Office for Europe are grateful to the staff of the Ministry of Health of Ukraine, the National Health Service of Ukraine, the Ministry of Finance of Ukraine, and the Statistical Services of Ukraine for assistance with access to data and feedback on findings during consultations prior to the finalization of this report.

The report was prepared under the overall leadership of Arup Banerji (the World Bank's Regional Country Director for Belarus, Moldova, and Ukraine) and Hans Kluge (the WHO Regional Director for Europe).

This report was prepared with co-financing from the Support to Reforms and Governance in the Health Sector in Ukraine project supported by the Swiss Agency for Development and Cooperation.

About the Authors

Caryn Bredenkamp is lead economist and program leader for human development for Eastern Europe (Belarus, Moldova, and Ukraine) at the World Bank's Kyiv, Ukraine, country office. She coordinates the World Bank's program in the health, education, and social protection sectors in Belarus, Moldova, and Ukraine and leads key sectoral dialogue with government counterparts, civil society, and development partners. Since joining the World Bank in 2006, Bredenkamp has worked on complex sectoral reform programs and lending activities in human development across diverse client countries in Africa, East Asia, Eastern Europe, and South Asia. She has worked most extensively in the Republic of Congo, India, the Philippines (where she completed field-based assignments), Myanmar, and Vietnam. Her expertise lies in health sector reforms that enhance efficiency and sustainability, improve financial protection, and promote equity and in bringing together multisectoral interventions to improve human capital outcomes. Before joining the World Bank, Bredenkamp was a lecturer in economics at the University of KwaZulu-Natal, South Africa. Her publications include more than 20 peer-reviewed journal articles and books. She holds a PhD in public policy (health economics) from the University of North Carolina–Chapel Hill (US), a master's degree in economics and a bachelor's degree in economics and political science from the University of Stellenbosch (South Africa), and postgraduate qualifications in demography and international health.

Elina Dale is a health financing specialist with 15 years of experience in policy analysis, research in global health, and the design and implementation of reforms to strengthen health systems. As a senior adviser to the global health team at the Norwegian Institute of Public Health (NIPH), her current work focuses on procedural fairness in health financing decisions. She also leads NIPH's collaboration on public health with the Public Health Centre of Ukraine. Before joining the NIPH, Dale served as a health policy adviser at the World Health Organization (WHO) country office in Ukraine, leading policy dialogue with the government of Ukraine on health system reform issues and supporting Ukraine's COVID-19 (coronavirus) response. Previously, she worked at the WHO Headquarters in Geneva, where she focused on fiscal space for health, budget reforms, and provider payment methods in countries including Armenia, Peru, and Tanzania. Before her doctoral studies, Dale worked in the Health Policy Analysis Unit under the Kyrgyz Ministry of Health, providing financial management support and conducting operational research on health system reforms in the country. Dale holds a PhD from the Johns Hopkins School of Public Health (US). Her dissertation focused on health worker motivation, quality of care, and performance-based financing in Afghanistan, where she conducted research between 2010 and 2013.

Olena Doroshenko is a senior health economist at the World Bank's Kyiv, Ukraine, country office. She leads programs in Belarus and Ukraine, supporting development of country health systems through investment projects and technical assistance, and supports teams working in other countries in Central Asia and Europe. In Ukraine, she coordinates large health system modernization projects and Ukraine's COVID-19 (coronavirus) emergency response operation, which has helped the country implement historic health reforms, develop primary care, and modernize acute care delivery during the pandemic. Doroshenko also manages technical assistance support to local governments, which covers health financing, public health activities, mental health, hospital reform, eHealth, and telemedicine among other important aspects of health system modernization. She holds an MSc in health policy, economics, and management from Maastricht University (Netherlands) and a PhD in public administration from the National Academy for Public Administration (Ukraine).

Yuriy Dzhygyr is a World Bank consultant working in Kyiv, Ukraine. He contributes to the World Bank's ongoing programs in health and social protection sectors, providing technical expertise, diagnostic analysis, and assistance in production of policy recommendations. His latest work focused on assessing progress and designing options for strengthening Ukraine's health financing reform, incorporating lessons from the COVID-19 (coronavirus) pandemic, and developing a resilience framework for Ukraine's human capital development in the areas of health care and social protection. Dzhygyr's expertise lies in public financial management, government spending policies in the human development sector, and fiscal decentralization. Before joining the World Bank, Dzhygyr was Ukraine's deputy Minister of Finance, responsible for public spending on human capital development programs. He was part of the team working on developing Ukraine's health financing reform in 2016–17. His background includes providing advice in public finance and decentralized expenditure management to governments in Ukraine, the Western Balkans, Central Asia, and East Asia and Pacific. Dzhygyr holds a master's degree in economics from the Maxwell School of Syracuse University (US), bachelor's degrees in economics and political science from the National University of Kyiv-Mohyla Academy (Ukraine), and postgraduate qualifications in macroeconomics, public sector debt management, financial development and financial inclusion, health system financing, epidemiology, and public health.

Jarno Habicht is a World Health Organization (WHO) representative and has been head of the Ukraine country office since November 2018. He previously was the WHO representative and head of country office in the Kyrgyz Republic (2015–18) and in Moldova (2011–15). He has worked for WHO since 2003 at the country level and is involved in international initiatives on health systems and public health. Habicht has served as a health specialist for the Estonian Health Insurance Fund and earlier was a consultant for various health projects and health information initiatives of the Estonian Department of Public Health (University of Tartu) and Ministry of Social Affairs, among others. He has authored approximately 50 peer-reviewed journal articles and books. Habicht holds an MD and PhD in medicine from the University of Tartu (Estonia).

Loraine Hawkins is a technical expert consultant on health financing, health systems, governance, and the interface between the health system and public financial management for the World Health Organization (WHO) Regional Office for Europe and the WHO Ukraine country office and is based in London, UK. She currently works on WHO's support to the National Health Service of Ukraine and the Ukraine Ministry of Health, focusing on development and adaptation of the Programme of Medical Guarantees, decentralization and health, and public financial management and health. She works in a similar role for WHO in Uzbekistan. Hawkins is a director of the Health Foundation, a health policy think tank in the UK. Over the past 25 years, she has worked in the same role for WHO and as a lead health specialist for the World Bank in the Baltic states, Armenia, Azerbaijan, Arab Republic of Egypt, Georgia, the Kyrgyz Republic, the Philippines, and Romania. She has worked in health systems in postconflict settings for the World Bank in Afghanistan, Bosnia and Herzegovina, Kosovo, Lebanon, North Macedonia, and Serbia and for the United Nations Children's Fund in Cambodia and the Lao People's Democratic Republic. She was chief analyst at National Health Service England from 2014 to 2016. Hawkins holds an MPA in economics and public policy from Princeton University (US) and a bachelor's degree in medical sciences and philosophy from the University of Otago (New Zealand).

Alexandr Katsaga is a WHO international consultant in health financing and health information systems areas and is based in Toronto, Canada. He supports the Ukraine Ministry of Health and National Health Service in implementing health purchasing reforms and developing the Program of Medical Guarantees in Ukraine. Katsaga has worked for different international organizations (including the European Union, the United States Agency for International Development, and the World Bank) in Africa, Central Asia, Eastern Europe, and Latin America and has participated in developing large-scale, country-level health policy strategies and reform programs and provider payment methods for hospital services. He has also provided training programs for various levels of health care management. Katsaga participated in the design of cost-analysis projects in the hospital sector in several countries and uses advanced analytical skills and business intelligence technologies in his work, including modeling various reform scenarios and possible management and policy decisions. He is an author or coauthor of numerous publications and research articles that focus on financing methods, development of monitoring systems, and other issues related to the reform of health care systems in several countries.

Kateryna Maynzyuk is a World Bank consultant working in Kyiv, Ukraine, providing technical analysis and advice to government counterparts and development partners in health financing and human development. She contributed to the World Bank's ongoing work to further health financing reform in Ukraine, to review government health expenditures, and to strengthen the resilience of Ukraine's human capital development systems. Maynzyuk's expertise is in public financial management, health care financing and social policy, and fiscal decentralization. Before joining the Work Bank, Maynzyuk worked as a consultant in public finance reforms advising government partners in Ukraine, the Western Balkans, Central Asia, and East Asia and Pacific. In Ukraine, she advised the Ministry of Health in designing the country's health care financing reform and worked with the Ministry of Finance to strengthen public expenditure management and spending efficiency in Human Capital Development programs. She holds an MSc in development studies (specializing in economics) from the London School of Economics and Political Science (UK) and a BA in economics (minor in sociology) from the National University of Kyiv-Mohyla Academy (Ukraine).

Khrystyna Pak is a World Bank consultant based in Lviv, Ukraine. She joined the World Bank team after successful technical implementation of a regional subproject on breast and cervical screening within the Serving People Improving Health Project. Before joining the World Bank, Pak worked for more than 10 years in municipal government administration, leading the economic direction as deputy head of the department and head of the analysis and strategic planning unit that covered the main activities of city administration, such as budgeting, planning, investing, regulations, local taxes, strategies, effective performance of different departments, communal enterprises, and local representatives of central government branches. She also worked closely with European Union projects in energy efficiency as a financial expert and with nongovernmental organizations as a consultant in local budgeting. Over the past 7 years, Pak's core field of work was linked to the health care sector. She holds a master's degree in public health from Uzhhorod National University (Ukraine), a master's degree in international economy and a bachelor's degree in economics of enterprises from Lviv Polytechnic National University, and a law degree from Ivan Franko National University of Lviv.

Olga Zues is a senior health economist at Abt Associates based in the United Kingdom. She has more than 20 years of experience working in international development as a health economist, technical director, and chief of party for the health system strengthening projects in Azerbaijan, Ghana, Kazakhstan, the Kyrgyz Republic, Tajikistan, Turkmenistan, Ukraine, and Uzbekistan. Her technical expertise includes the design and implementation of comprehensive reform strategies to strengthen health systems, benefits design to move toward universal health coverage, arrangements to support efficiency gains and service delivery improvements, innovative payment mechanisms, sustainability strategies, and institutional development. During 2018–20, Zues worked for the World Health Organization and supported the Ukraine Ministry of Health and National Health Service in the implementation of health purchasing reforms. She has extensive experience working with development partners and national governments.

Executive Summary

This report reviews the progress of the implementation of health financing reform in Ukraine, in particular the funding, purchasing, and governance of the Program of Medical Guarantees (PMG). The health care reforms initiated in 2015 culminated in the Law on Financial Guarantees for Health Care Services, which define a guaranteed benefit package—the PMG—for all Ukrainians and created the National Health Service of Ukraine (NHSU) to serve as the strategic purchaser for this program. The vision was that the PMG would expand over time to eventually cover all types of health care and that financing would evolve from input-based to output-based modalities to better align the provision of care with patient needs. In 2019, a joint World Health Organization (WHO)–World Bank review took stock of reform progress since 2017. Many important developments, including the COVID-19 (coronavirus) shock, have taken place since then, warranting a new assessment of where things stand and what future directions should be.

Tremendous progress has been made in consolidating previously fragmented sources of government health financing into one program—the PMG. By end-2020, 68 percent of total government health spending had been consolidated within the PMG. Subnational governments (SNGs) still play an important role in financing, however, as they are responsible for financing the utility costs of the communal health facilities that they own and may also provide supplemental resources for current and capital costs. As resources—and willingness to use them for health care—vary across localities, SNG financing is also a source of inequity. To reduce it, the government could consider including facility utility costs in the PMG. In addition, the funding of quaternary health facilities could be integrated into the PMG.

The PMG has the potential to reduce "catastrophic" out-of-pocket spending on health, but refinement of the benefit package and additional resources to deliver it are needed. Catastrophic health spending—which occurs when a household devotes more than 10 percent of its consumption to health care—is usually associated with the use of inpatient care. Since 2020, inpatient care has been included in the PMG, which, in principle, means that it is provided free of charge at contracted facilities. However, the political and technical process for the design, expansion, budgeting, and approval of the PMG benefit package is too broadly defined and not fully transparent. As a result, the PMG cannot realistically be delivered within current budget constraints. In 2021, for example, the Ministry of Health (MoH) and the NHSU requested three times more financing than what was eventually allocated to the PMG.

Because the benefit package that is guaranteed to the population is not yet fully funded, services are rationed at the point of care (or paid for informally). Of the six options for expanding financing for the PMG discussed in the report—increasing taxes, reprioritizing government spending toward health, reprioritizing spending within the health sector, increasing the efficiency of the health sector, pooling some local government spending with the PMG, and introducing cost-sharing—the one that has the greatest potential is reforms that enhance the efficiency of the health sector. Efficiency-enhancing reforms include reducing the excessive reliance on costly hospital care, strengthening primary health care (PHC), and shifting to payment approaches that better incentivize the effective use of resources.

In 2020, the PMG was expanded to include 31 packages of services, including 4 new packages designed to provide COVID-19-specific care. New, specialized care packages included care provided by hospitals (inpatient and outpatient), clinical-diagnostic centers, specialized mono-profile outpatient clinics, and emergency medical services. In response to the COVID-19 pandemic, four packages—covering testing by mobile brigades, prehospital emergency care, hospitalization, and a COVID-related salary top-up—were added to the PMG in mid-2020. In 2021, a COVID-19 vaccination package was added. Although the scope and tariff of packages are more clearly defined than in 2020, some packages are still not as clearly defined as they need to be.

The purchasing of PHC, which is based on age-adjusted capitation payments to contracted providers, has proven to be effective and sustainable. It continues to evolve. Enrollment with contracted PHC providers has expanded to cover over 70 percent of the population. The participation of private providers has also increased; they now account for almost a third of the 1,696 providers of PHC in Ukraine. Digital technologies have been exploited to introduce e-referrals for patients requiring nonemergency specialized care, and e-prescriptions are used within the Affordable Medicines Program (AMP). In 2021, additional services (covering tuberculosis, mental health, and COVID-19 vaccination) were added to the PHC package, and performance-based payments for select quality indicators were introduced. The AMP, which is now integrated into the PMG and administered by the NHSU, gives 2.8 million Ukrainians access to medicines with no or a small copayment (through direct reimbursement of contracted pharmacies within the PMG). There is room to expand the types of medicines included in the AMP, but the first priority should be to address the geographic inequities in access caused by the small number of participating pharmacies in some localities.

The introduction of new payment approaches for inpatient care has generated a wealth of experience on which Ukraine should continue to build. Like PHC providers, providers of hospital care are now contracted, which means that funding is available only to facilities that meet contractual requirements (staffing, equipment, infrastructure, and willingness to provide care according to the protocols defined for each package within the PMG). Global budget financing (linked to performance indicators, morbidity, and capacity of providers) was used to purchase 81 percent of the specialized care in the PMG in 2020

(67 percent of the total PMG budget). Fee-for-service is used for select diagnostic and treatment procedures. Since March 2020, case-based payments (specifically diagnosis-related groups [DRGs]) have been used to pay for four types of care: acute stroke, myocardial infarction, childbirth, and complex neonatal care. These payments accounted for 8.1 percent of PMG financing in 2020. Case-based payments were intended to be introduced for all inpatient care in March 2020, but under the pressures and uncertainties of the COVID-19 pandemic, full implementation was postponed; implementation commenced in April 2021. Before it was implemented, hospitals reported cases to the NHSU using DRGs, an important building block for DRG implementation.

The governance arrangements of the PMG need strengthening. Five aspects of governance—autonomy of the purchasing agency, clarity in roles and methodologies, effective interagency coordination, external accountability, and internal control—are essential. The roles and processes of all agencies involved in implementing the PMG, at both the national level (the MoH, the NHSU, the Ministry of Finance [MoF], and the Cabinet of Ministers [CabMin]) and the regional level (the NHSU subnational offices, subnational administrations, and hospital district councils) need to be better defined if all agencies are to function and cooperate effectively. In addition, it is important that the recent transformation of health facilities into autonomous enterprises be supported with additional regulations to improve their internal governance and external accountability. A prerequisite for better governance is adequate capacity of the MoH and the NHSU, as well as the agencies to which they are accountable, in terms of personnel, information technology (IT), and other resources.

Concurrent developments in the health sector have bolstered implementation of the PMG. The "hub hospitals" that will form part of the Capable Network,[1] where service delivery reforms will be concentrated, have been identified, laying the foundation for greater efficiency in service delivery. The e-health system has become more sophisticated and now includes electronic health records and referrals, creating the potential for better coordination of patient pathways. A stronger e-health and claims reporting system would also enable the NHSU to better understand provider and patient behaviors and monitor records for potential fraud. The continued complementarity of health financing reform and other sectoral policies will be important as Ukraine develops its new long-term strategic vision for universal health care. A clearly defined service delivery model and benefit package are needed that are responsive to people's needs, with financing and purchasing arrangements to support this vision.

This report makes recommendations in three areas, which can be summarized as follows:

1. **Improving the Funding of the PMG Benefit Package**

- Clarify the political and technical process for the design, expansion, and approval of the PMG benefit package to make it explicit, more transparent, and participatory.
- Increase public spending on health in line with economic growth and increases in general government spending, in order to realize the coverage and financial protection goals of the PMG.
- Ensure full commitment to current tax reform roadmaps, in particular the tobacco tax roadmap, which envisions a gradual increase in line with the EU–Ukraine Association Agreement.

- Increase spending efficiency by accelerating hospital right-sizing and network rationalization, gradually introducing case-rate payments, and strengthening and better integrating PHC.
- Consider shifting financing responsibilities for utilities from SNGs to the PMG budget in order to reduce inefficiencies, help "money-follow-the-patient," and reduce inequities across providers.
- Prepare a long-term health financing strategy that includes a vision for expanding the PMG program and its financing, as well as complementary policies, over a 10-year period.

2. Improving the Purchasing of PMG Services

Primary Health Care

- Articulate and approve a long-term strategic vision for PHC, with a clearly defined service delivery model that is responsive to people's needs and purchasing arrangements to support it.
- Introduce and mandate the use of standardized clinical protocols within the PMG at the PHC level, starting with priority conditions (such as major noncommunicable diseases).
- Accelerate the use of digital technologies in health care delivery across a broad range of functions, from further development of the e-health architecture to implementation of telemedicine.
- Introduce a performance monitoring framework for PHC to measure performance across facilities and within facilities over time, in order to improve accountability for the delivery of quality care.

The Affordable Medicines Program

- Update the Essential Medicines List (EML), on which the AMP draws, to ensure that the medicines included are aligned with modern clinical guidelines and are cost-effective.
- Assess the trade-offs between including more conditions and medicines in the AMP and ensuring sufficient funding for less costly and more cost-effective medicines (with the latter as priority).
- Encourage the expansion of AMP–contracted pharmacies in underserved regions and underserved areas within each region, to help reduce geographic imbalances.
- Explore the potential for the NHSU to monitor prescribing behavior, using the e-prescription and e-health system, not only to detect fraud but also to improve the clinical appropriateness of care.

Specialized Outpatient, Prehospital Emergency, and Hospital Care

- Define more explicitly the PMG packages and further unbundle the 131 Ukrainian Diagnosis-Related Groups (UDRGs) used to pay for them, in order to increase clinical and cost homogeneity, thus reducing the financial risk to providers.
- Lay out a clear transition pathway toward DRG payments that provides facilities time to adjust and gives protection against excessive financial risk.
- Replace annual and selective contracting (in which providers choose which packages they deliver) with multiyear, comprehensive contracts in order to guarantee equitable access to all PMG services.

- Review the Capable Network Plan to ensure a more transparent hospital selection methodology in which inclusion criteria are aligned with policy principles.
- Continue to strengthen the use of NHSU data for decision-making, not only for claims review and fraud detection but also for policy development.

3. Improving the Governance of PMG Services

- Create a CabMin committee to facilitate coordination and consensus across the MoF, the MoH, the NHSU, and other ministries on PMG scope, budget, and tariffs.
- As part of broader public sector governance reform toward performance-based monitoring, consider piloting a mechanism for results-reporting to the CabMin on NHSU performance.
- Develop an NHSU organizational strategy, aligned with the health financing strategy, with performance objectives and indicators.
- Establish a small permanent unit in the MoH with technical expertise in health financing policy, to enable the MoH to better perform its stewardship and governance roles with respect to the NHSU.
- Further specify the role and procedures of the Public Control Council (PCC) with respect to NHSU governance, including the information and reports the NHSU should provide to the PCC.

NOTE

1. The MoH identified 212 hospitals that are included in the Capable Network for inpatient care. The Capable Network Plan was approved by the Cabinet of Ministers of Ukraine in January 2020.

Abbreviations

ALOS	average length of stay
AMP	Affordable Medicines Program
CabMin	Cabinet of Ministers
CEA	Central Executive Agency
COVID-19	coronavirus (pandemic)
CVD	cardiovascular disease
DRG	diagnosis-related group
EML	Essential Medicines List
EU	European Union
GDP	gross domestic product
HEUS	Health Expenditure and Utilization Survey
HTA	Health Technology Assessment
IMF	International Monetary Fund
INN	international nonproprietary name
MoF	Ministry of Finance
MoH	Ministry of Health
NCD	noncommunicable disease
NHA	National Health Accounts
NHSU	National Health Service of Ukraine
OECD	Organisation for Economic Co-operation and Development
OOP	out-of-pocket
PCC	Public Control Council
PFM	Public Financial Management
PHC	primary health care
PMG	Program of Medical Guarantees
SNG	subnational government
TB	tuberculosis
UAH	Ukrainian hryvnia (national currency)
UDRG	Ukrainian diagnosis-related group
WHO	World Health Organization

1 Introduction

In 2015, the government of Ukraine initiated fundamental reform of its health system, with the goals of improving the health outcomes of the population and providing financial protection from excessive out-of-pocket health care payments. The reforms were to be implemented by modernizing and integrating the service delivery system, introducing changes to provider payment arrangements that incentivize efficiency, and improving the quality of care. They culminated in the passage of a new health financing law—the Law on Financial Guarantees for Health Care Services 2017—which established a health benefit package called the Program of Medical Guarantees (PMG) and created the National Health Service of Ukraine (NHSU) to serve as strategic purchaser for this program. The vision was that the PMG would expand over time to eventually cover all types of care and that financing would evolve from input-based to output-based modalities to better align the provision of care with patient need.

In 2019, the World Health Organization (WHO) and the World Bank published a review of the reforms. It took stock of reform progress since 2017, highlighting achievements, identifying challenges, and providing recommendations on how to overcome them. The report examined five areas: governance; financing (fiscal space, revenue collection, pooling arrangements); strategic purchasing of primary health care (PHC); preparation for strategic purchasing at the hospital level; and the design of the benefit package.

Two years later, implementation of health financing reforms has progressed substantially, and it is time to again review where things stand and what future directions should be. There have been many important accomplishments over the last two years, in terms of both institutional reform and expansion of access to care. Primary care enrollment has increased to include more than 70 percent of the population. The Affordable Medicines Program (AMP) has been integrated into the PMG and is now administered by the NHSU; some 2.8 million Ukrainians have already accessed medicines through it. In mid-2021, the government expanded the scope of the PMG to include specialized and emergency care, tuberculosis (TB) and mental health care, and COVID vaccination. Reform of the hospital payment system has also been initiated, and reporting of hospital cases by diagnosis-related group (DRG) in preparation for payment by DRGs has begun. The e-health system has become more sophisticated and now includes electronic health records and referrals. The "hub hospitals" that will form part of the Capable Network, where service delivery reforms will be concentrated, have been identified.

The COVID-19 pandemic precipitated adjustments to existing health financing levels and arrangements. These adjustments included the introduction of new services packages for treatment, testing, COVID-related emergency care, and vaccination as well as short-term salary top-ups for staff working at facilities designated for COVID-19 care. The pandemic also delayed implementation of some aspects of the health financing reforms, such as the anticipated transition to case-based payments.

This report provides a comprehensive description and assessment of the development and implementation of policies associated with the PMG reform, from the start of reform in 2017 through mid-2021. It examines (a) how the PMG is financed (levels, trends, budgetary processes, and options for increasing its financing); (b) the governance arrangements of the PMG; and (c) strategic purchasing of the different components of the PMG benefit package (PHC, medicines, and specialized [emergency, inpatient, and outpatient] care). It positions these developments within broader contextual discussions of the financing and organization of health care in Ukraine, in order to make the key features of financing reforms and their importance accessible to domestic and international audiences. Adjustment by the health sector to cope with the COVID-19 pandemic is a common thread. Each section concludes with a set of recommendations.

FUNDING THE PMG BENEFIT PACKAGE

The 2017 health reform pooled most of government health care spending into a single central program—the PMG, which is administered by the NHSU and is provided free of charge to the population through contracted health facilities. The PMG transformed the previous vague constitutional commitment to free health care for all into an entitlement to a defined package of health services. It reduced the fragmentation of health financing and shifted responsibility for government spending from hundreds of subnational governments (SNGs), which were previously responsible for most operational costs, to the national government. SNGs retain responsibility for the utility costs of local health facilities. They also have the option to supplement the operational budget of their facilities. This option provides facilities with a buffer against potential revenue shortfalls, but it weakens the incentive for them to become more efficient, contributing to horizontal inequities in health care financing.

PMG funding: levels, trends, and budgetary process

By the end of 2020, the PMG accounted for 68 percent of consolidated government health spending. About 53 percent of total spending was pooled in the PMG and financed by the central government; 9 percent was paid by SNGs to cover specialized and emergency care services during the first quarter of 2020, before these services were included in the PMG; 6 percent was spent by SNGs on capital investments; and 6 percent was spent by SNGs to cover the utility costs associated with the PMG (figure 1.1). The PMG will grow further as more specialized curative services are absorbed into it, leaving mainly preventive, administrative, and research activities funded by the central and subnational governments.[1]

The PMG was introduced in order to ensure equitable access to care and provide financial protection from the costs associated with seeking care, which have historically been high in Ukraine. Ukrainians face high out-of-pocket (OOP) spending on health, which increased from 38.0 percent of total health spending in 2005 to 49.3 percent in 2018. This share is much larger than the average for other lower-middle-income countries (38.4 percent), although it is similar to the average for lower-middle-income countries in the European region (50.6 percent) (figure 1.2).[2] With the rollout of the PMG to specialized curative care (mainly hospitals) in April 2020, it is still too early to assess its full effect on OOP. However, as most OOP is spent on medicines and medical goods (74.9 percent in 2018, according to the Ukraine National Health Accounts, prepared by the State Statistical Services of Ukraine), the 2020 expansion of the PMG is unlikely to have a significant impact on aggregate OOP spending, except to the extent that pharmaceuticals are included in inpatient curative care packages or can be purchased at pharmacies through the AMP.

The PMG could help reduce the incidence of catastrophic health care spending, which tends to be associated with unpredictable and extended use of inpatient care. The incidence of catastrophic spending in Ukraine rose over the last decade. Between 2010 and 2019, the share of the population spending more than 10 percent of its total consumption on health care grew from 6.9 percent to 7.8 percent, and the share of households whose health care spending exceeded

FIGURE 1.1

Consolidated health spending: PMG, Central, and Local—2020 plan, June 2020

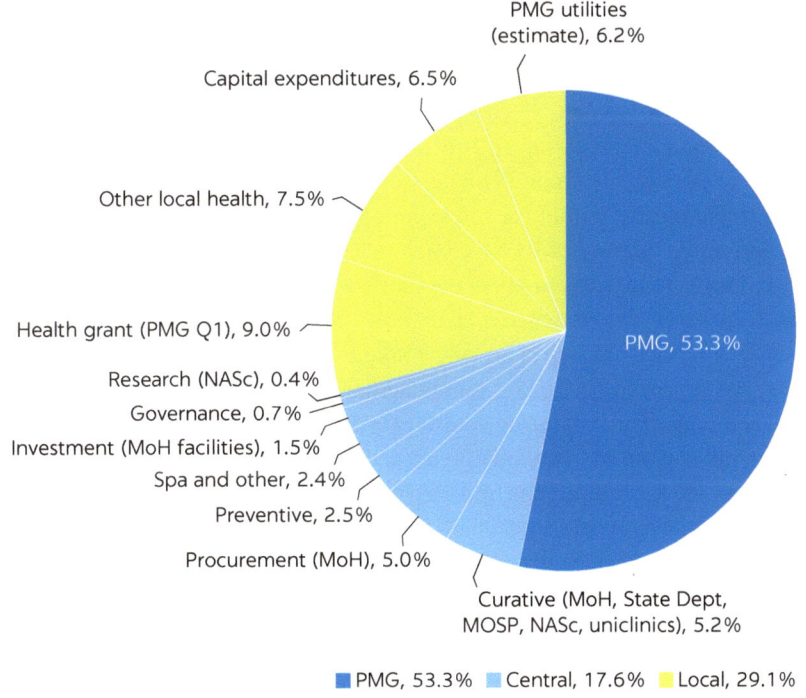

Source: State Treasury Service of Ukraine.
Note: MoH = Ministry of Health; MOSP = Ministry of Social Policy; NASc = National Academy of Sciences; PMG = Program of Medical Guarantees; Q1 = first quarter; Spa = facilities providing spa services, which include a medical component to support treatment and rehabilitation of the patients.

FIGURE 1.2

Out-of-pocket spending as share of total current health spending in Ukraine and selected country groups, 2000–18

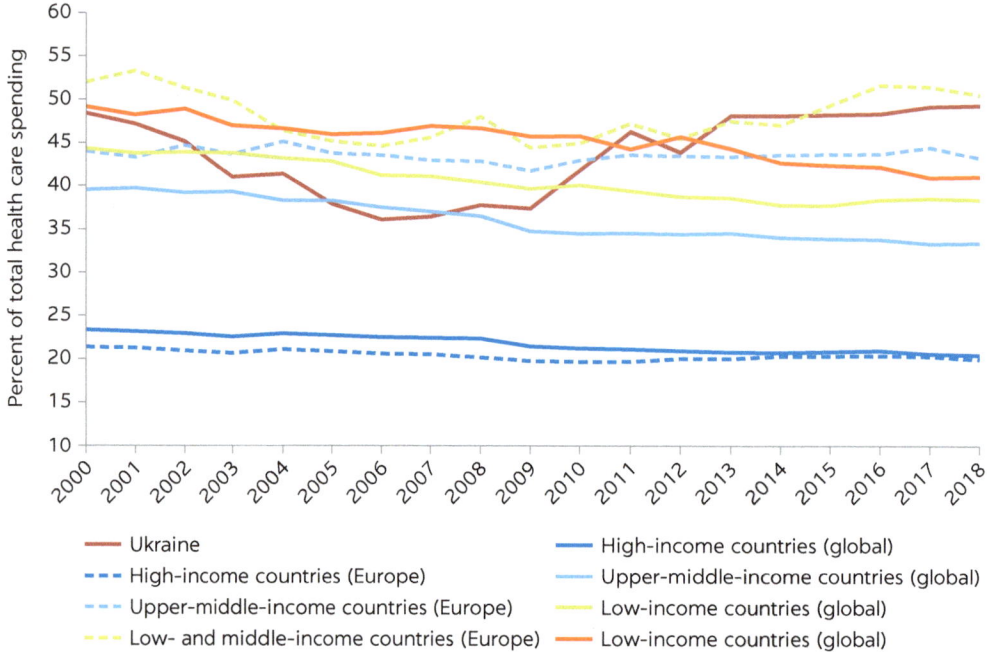

Sources: State Statistics Service of Ukraine (for Ukraine); World Development Indicators database; Global Health Expenditure Database.
Note: Regional averages are population-weighted.

WHO Europe's "capacity to pay" threshold increased from 11.5 percent to 16.7 percent.[3] Catastrophic spending is heavily concentrated in the bottom consumption quintile. The PMG can also potentially address the large unmet need for health care, which has grown by a factor of 1.4 since 2009, to affect an average of 24.5 percent of households in 2017 and 2018, according to the State Statistics Service of Ukraine's Household Living Conditions Surveys.

In recent years, the political and technical processes for determining, updating, and budgeting the PMG have been marked by increasing discretion and decreasing transparency. In 2020, the Law on Financial Guarantees for Health Care Services 2017 was revised such that the PMG benefit package specification (including service pricing) is no longer voted on by the Parliament (*Verkhovna Rada*) and approved as part of the annual Budget Law but is instead approved at the discretion of the Cabinet of Ministers (CabMin). The rules for the technical development of the PMG are very broad, and the methodology of the Ministry of Health (MoH) for defining and updating the National Health Priorities on which the PMG is based is not made public, giving the MoH wide discretion in defining the scope of the PMG and preventing scrutiny of its decisions. In particular, PMG costing and pricing processes lack clear and transparent methodologies.

A compounding challenge is the government-wide, medium-term budgeting process. This process was introduced in 2018 but suspended in 2020. As result, the CabMin did not approve the planned three-year horizon for PMG development. It could be argued that this decision was an appropriate pandemic response, providing the government with flexibility in a rapidly changing environment. But it also created uncertainty about the future of PMG package development.

For the 2021 budget, the MoH and the NHSU requested funding equivalent to 6 percent of gross domestic product (GDP), almost three times as much as was budgeted for the PMG in the 2020 amended budget. Although not a realistic budget expectation, this request was indicative of the intention to continue to implement the shift from supply-side to demand-side financing that "follows the patient" and provides an increasingly generous benefit package over time. In the approved 2021 budget, NHSU expenditures on the PMG were approved at a level that represents a 2.3 percent increase over the amount approved in 2020.

Options for increasing the funding allocated to the PMG

It is vital that the annual budget allocations to the PMG be sufficient to cover the provision of services included by law in the PMG benefit package; if they are not, service rationing will be necessary, undermining the guarantee to care provided by the government to the Ukrainian people. Six options could be considered for finding the resources to expand the PMG, as envisaged as part of the reform process. Not all of them are likely to be equally effective in terms of revenue generation prospects, and some (such as cost-sharing) may entail risks for health sector goals of access and financial protection. The six options are as follows:

1. *Expanding the fiscal envelope through higher growth and increased tax revenues.* Stronger growth and higher revenues could be a potential source of additional resources for the health sector. Prospects for this option appear limited, however. In the past, procyclical fiscal policies in Ukraine led to the accumulation of large macroeconomic imbalances, requiring debt restructuring in 2015. Following a sustained period of fiscal consolidation, the fiscal deficit increased to 6 percent of GDP in 2020, in large part because of COVID–related outlays, including for medical procurement, higher wages for health workers, and pension top-ups. Fiscal financing needs were estimated at 16 percent of GDP in 2021 (up from 15 percent in 2020), partly because large debt repayments on past borrowing were coming due. Ukraine's external public debt service burden is expected to average about US$10 billion a year during 2020–25, up from less than US$6 billion a year over 2015–19.[4] Medium-term spending pressures, related to large minimum wage increases and pension spending, are also increasing. Fiscal contingent liabilities are large, particularly in the energy sector, and will eventually have to be recognized. In addition, new sources of fiscal risk have emerged, related to GDP-linked guarantees that may potentially lead to large fiscal costs and exceed the initial debt write-off when certain growth thresholds are exceeded. There is some scope for additional revenue mobilization measures—through better tax and customs collection or pro-health taxes on sugar and tobacco, for example. However, Ukraine already collects significantly more taxes than its regional peers, with total tax collection averaging 35 percent of GDP over the last five years, compared with a 22 percent regional average. This rate of tax collection is higher than the average for upper-middle-income countries and some high-income countries in the region. Together, these factors point to constrained fiscal space in the medium term. They will require strong control over expenditure pressures and fiscal deficits to keep Ukraine on a sustainable macro-fiscal path.

2. *Reprioritizing across sectors within the existing fiscal envelope.* Within the constrained fiscal envelope, another opportunity for finding resources to expand the PMG would be to reprioritize government spending toward health. Since 2014, the share of health in the government budget has been falling. After remaining at about 12 percent between 2007 and 2013, it fell to 9 percent in 2016, remaining there through 2020. Combined with the reduction in general government spending, the decline meant that health expenditures decreased to 3.2 percent of GDP in 2016 and remained at about 3 percent in subsequent years, including in the initial 2020 budget allocation (figure 1.3). The 2020 COVID-19 budget amendments increased the share of the government budget allocated to health to 10.4 percent (4.2 percent of GDP)—the largest share since 2007. On top of this, the 2021 budget plan[5] increased central spending on health, including transfers to local governments, to 12.1 percent of total government spending (3.6 percent of GDP).[6] Comparisons with countries in the Organisation for Economic Co-operation and Development (OECD) and European Union (EU) suggest that there may still be room to increase the share of the government budget going to health, as the health spending share in Ukraine as of early 2020 was only about 40 percent the 2019 OECD average (partly because Ukraine allocates a much larger budgetary share to internal security, social protection, and education than the OECD average). The health spending share in Ukraine is relatively high for countries at a similar level of income globally, however (8.9 percent in Ukraine compared with an average of 5.0 percent for all lower-middle-income countries), and it is in line with lower-middle-income countries in the European region (9.3 percent). The way to determine whether there is room to further prioritize health in the government budget would be to conduct a whole-of-government spending review that identifies spending needs across functions, detects inefficiencies, and evaluates possibilities for resource allocation, taking into consideration the medium-term macro-fiscal outlook.

FIGURE 1.3

Health spending as a share of total spending and GDP, 2007–20

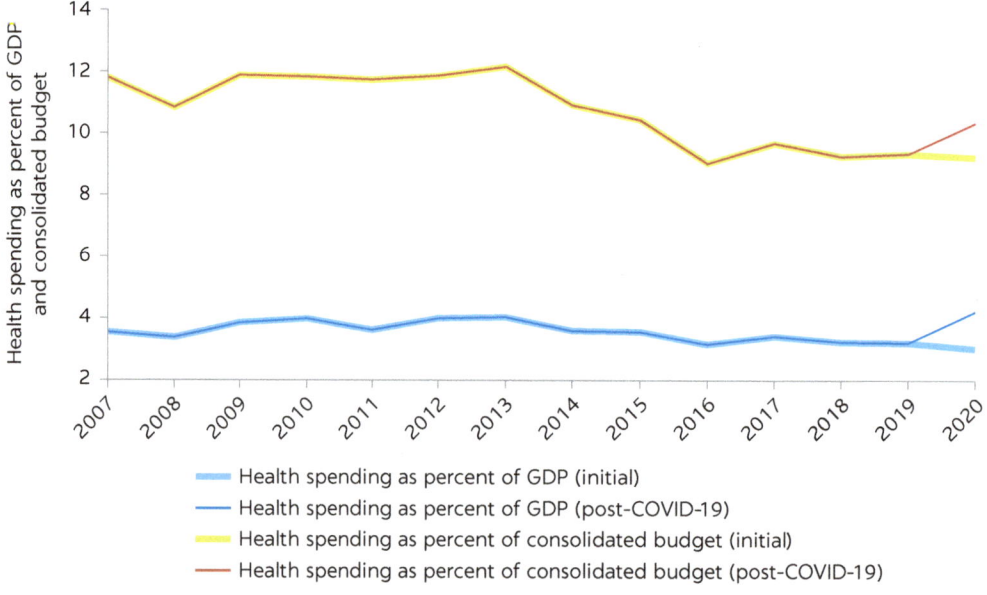

Sources: State Treasury Service of Ukraine; State Statistics Service of Ukraine.
Note: COVID-19 = coronavirus (pandemic).

3. *Reprioritizing within the health sector.* The health sector needs to decide what priority to give to the PMG versus other health programs. It is highly unlikely that other health programs can be substantially cut back without adverse consequences for population health. Therefore, expanding the PMG beyond the current 68 percent of the consolidated health budget spent on the services it covers, including utility and capital costs paid by the SNGs and not pooled within the NHSU, does not seem possible. However, it is possible that detailed sectoral spending reviews could identify potential savings within the health budget that could free up resources for other areas of health spending, such as the PMG. The MoH should therefore regularly conduct such reviews. Looking ahead, there is likely to be an apparent increase in the PMG's share of consolidated health spending, as a further 5 percent of the health budget currently spent on highly specialized (quaternary) curative services is intended to be migrated to the PMG at some point as part of the envisioned reform. This change will merely reclassify some expenditures, though; it will not increase the PMG budget.

4. *Introducing sectoral reforms that enable more efficient use of the existing PMG budget.* Ukraine can achieve significantly better health outcomes by removing inefficiencies in the way the government spends the PMG budget. These inefficiencies are not related to the PMG itself but to broader health sector policies on the organization of the health services the PMG funds. This issue is discussed in detail in the section "Purchasing PMG Services" below and in chapter 3. One such inefficiency is the excessive reliance on costly hospital care and the resulting problem of redundant and inefficient hospital networks. For example, there is scope for efficiency gains in reforming rural hospitals and obstetric care, where low occupancy has not yet triggered the needed reorganization, and in inpatient TB care, which accommodates patients well beyond the intensive care period, including inactive TB. Hospitals in Ukraine are also very poorly equipped, and doctors perform fewer services and procedures than they do in comparator countries. The share of auxiliary personnel is larger in Ukraine than in EU countries, and no task-shifting strategy is in place to optimize workloads. Ukraine could also increase value-for-money in the PMG by further strengthening the role of PHC and effectively integrating care levels to prevent noncommunicable diseases and treat them earlier. Moving ahead with provider payment reforms, including the introduction of case rates for specialized care, would enhance the efficiency of the hospital system by providing a financial incentive to provide care at the most appropriate level and in the most cost-effective way (by, for example, reducing unnecessary admissions, shortening length of stay, and shifting care to the most appropriate level).

5. *Shifting spending from local governments to pooled spending through the NHSU.* Shifting the cost of utilities, which SNGs currently bear, to the central health budget would reduce some of the inefficiencies of the current arrangement, including the lack of managerial flexibility at the facility level in the use of the budget arising from line-item budgeting for utilities and complications in the costing of case rates when some components of the cost of care are paid from the PMG and others by SNGs. Shifting these costs would also address the uneven playing field for private providers that cover their own utility costs and public providers that vary in the extent of support they receive from their SNGs for utility costs. This measure would not expand the financing envelope available for PMG services; it would merely shift financing

responsibility from local governments and private providers to the national government.

6. *Introducing patient cost-sharing.* The government is considering introducing copayments for services covered by the PMG and supplementary payments for noncovered services in order to permit an expanded range of services and choice of amenities for people who can afford to pay more. Cost-sharing entails considerable risk of adverse consequences: it could increase Ukraine's already heavy reliance on OOPs through formal and informal payments, significantly increase administrative costs, and weaken strategic purchasing if not strictly regulated. It is not realistic to expect that the introduction of cost-sharing will permit the PMG to expand the range of services it covers without undermining the PMG's objective of ensuring equitable access to services. If cost-sharing is introduced, it should be in the form of small, flat copayments that are subject to annual caps and be limited to select services (excluding preventive care, in order to promote its utilization); poor households should be exempt from all copayments; and percentage copayments should be avoided. The design of any copayment policy should be as simple as possible, to ensure that people can easily navigate the health system and do not face administrative barriers to benefiting from protective measures. In addition to copayments for covered services, the government is considering allowing supplementary payments as a means of encouraging private providers to supply PMG services. If implemented, supplementary payments should be limited to aspects of service delivery that are not directly associated with the clinical quality of care, such as a single room in a hospital ("extra billing"). Health care providers should not be allowed to ask patients to pay a supplement in addition to copayments for covered services (also called "balance billing"). Implementation of copayments for covered services and supplementary payments for noncovered services requires careful regulation and active monitoring to avoid creating inequities (including potential discrimination against people who are exempt from copayments or do not make supplementary payments). If introduced, they will need to be accompanied by measures to reduce these risks.

Table 1.1 summarizes the prospects for revenue-raising through the six options.

Recommendations for improving the funding of the PMG benefit package

The analysis leads to the following recommendations:

- Clarify the political and technical process for the design, expansion, and approval of the PMG benefit package to make it explicit, more transparent, and participatory.
- Increase public spending on health in line with economic growth and increases in general government spending while also ensuring that in times of economic contraction, the current levels of public spending on health are protected in real per capita terms, in order to realize the coverage and financial protection goals to which the government committed when it passed the Law on the Financial Guarantees for Health Care Services.
- Ensure full commitment to current tax reform roadmaps, in particular the tobacco tax roadmap, which envisions a gradual increase in tobacco rates,

TABLE 1.1 **Prospects for increasing the resources allocated to fund the PMG**

OPTION	PROSPECTS	JUSTIFICATION FOR RATING
1. Expanding the fiscal envelope through economic growth and revenue collection	Low	Growth is low and the scope for introducing new taxes is limited.
2. Reprioritizing spending across sectors within the existing fiscal envelope	Medium	COVID–related adjustments aside, the health share of government spending and GDP is historically low. It is also low by OECD standards, although it is similar to spending in many middle-income countries in Europe and globally.
3. Reprioritizing spending within the health sector	Low	Cutting back funding on other health programs could have a detrimental effect on population health.
4. Introducing sectoral reforms that enable the existing PMG budget to be used more efficiently	High	Broader health sector policies on the organization and financing of services that are included in the PMG do not sufficiently incentivize efficient service delivery.
5. Shifting spending on components of cost of care from local governments to pooled spending through the NHSU	Low	Shifting spending would not increase fiscal resources, but it could contribute to greater equity in financing.
6. Increasing the patient's share of spending	Low	Once exemptions for poor people and priority services are in place, copayments would be small and potentially inequitable and inefficient.

Source: World Bank.
Note: GDP = gross domestic product; NHSU = National Health Service of Ukraine; OECD = Organisation for Economic Co-operation and Development; PMG = Program of Medical Guarantees.

in line with the EU–Ukraine Association Agreement, as well as broader revenue administration reform.

- Increase spending efficiency by accelerating hospital right-sizing and network rationalization, gradually introducing case-rate payments for inpatient care, and crafting a clear strategy for strengthening the role of PHC and integrated service provision.
- Consider shifting financing responsibilities for utilities from SNGs to the central budget—to be paid by the NHSU via the PMG budget to facilities—in order to reduce inefficiencies, strengthen the principle of "money-follows-the patient," and help level the playing field across providers.
- Prepare a long-term health financing strategy that can be politically endorsed and would include a vision for expanding the PMG program and financing it over a 10-year period; complementary plans for associated programs, such as the gradual expansion of the AMP to replace OOP spending on medicines; and policies such as stronger regulations to prevent overprescribing and improve health care quality.

PURCHASING PMG SERVICES

The NHSU purchases PMG services through service packages defined annually but adjusted throughout the year. In 2020, the PMG expanded from covering only PHC services to covering all types of care, including hospital and specialized outpatient care. It included 29 specialized care packages, 4 of which were developed in response to the COVID-19 pandemic, in addition to the PHC package and the AMP, for a total of 31 packages (figure 1.4). As of May 2021, there were 35 packages, but further changes were implemented in June, including the absorption of COVID-19-specific packages into other packages. Some PMG packages are very specifically defined (such as the packages for hemodialysis, colonoscopy, and acute stroke); others are very broadly defined (such as the single package for "all other types of secondary and tertiary outpatient care").

FIGURE 1.4

Service packages purchased under the PMG

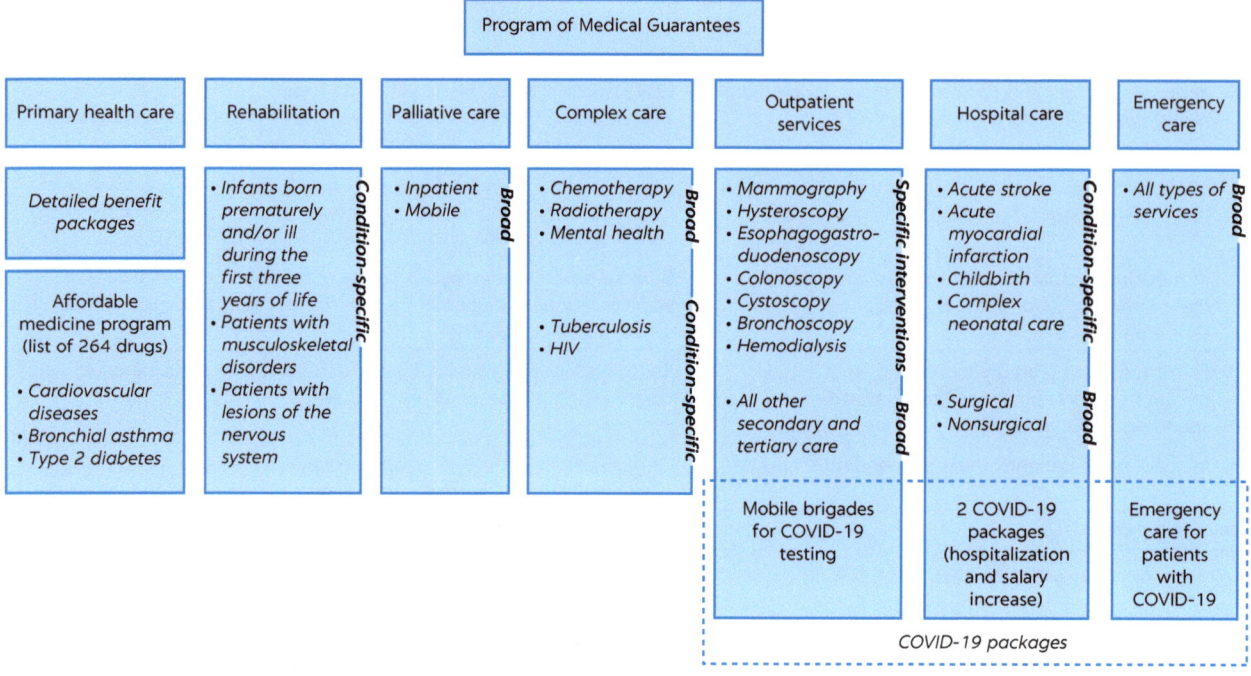

Source: World Bank.
Note: COVID-19 = coronavirus (pandemic).

The NHSU purchases services from providers using contracts that include a range of service specifications related to service organization, equipment, and personnel. A provider can apply to provide any one of the service packages, a practice that risks potential inequity in geographical access to services, with overconcentration in some areas and gaps in others. As contracting is not subject to a masterplan for a network of services, strategic purchasing through the NHSU can improve efficiency at the level of the individual provider but cannot make the provider network more efficient.

Services are purchased using different types of payment methods, including global budgets, case-based payments, fee-for-service for hospital care, and capitation for PHC. The parallel development of an e-health system, starting in 2018, has been a critical support for the purchasing function.

Primary health care

The scope and purchasing modalities for the PHC package have not changed substantially since the launch of PHC reform in 2018, except for an upward adjustment of capitation rates in late 2020 to compensate for sample collection for testing and teleconsultations related to COVID-19. PHC services included in the PMG are explicitly defined. The 17 service types include common diagnostics and treatments for acute and chronic conditions, preventive screening, vaccination, pregnancy and child health check-ups, and certain types of emergency and palliative care. By March 2021, the NHSU had contracted PMG services from 1,696 providers, 77 percent of which were PHC centers that consolidate multiple doctors and service delivery locations under one legal entity.

Thirty-five percent of contracted PHC providers are privately owned. All residents of Ukraine who have actively enrolled with a PHC physician contracted by the NHSU are eligible to receive care, and patients can change their provider at any time. By end-March 2021, 31.2 million people—70.3 percent of the population—had enrolled with a PHC provider. Providers are paid based on a national capitation rate adjusted for age and terrain that includes a penalty for providers that exceed the recommended number of people enrolled. In November 2020, the base capitation rate was increased by 8.5 percent as a COVID-19 adjustment, and PHC facilities became responsible for collecting samples for COVID-19 testing (but not the testing of the sample itself), which had previously been a separate COVID-19 package delivered through mobile teams operating from specialized outpatient care departments or PHC centers. In 2021, PHC providers became eligible to apply to deliver the COVID-19 vaccination package, which could be a source of additional revenue for them. For patients, PHC services are free at the point of care, but patients might still make informal payments to providers.

PHC providers are beginning to play an important gatekeeping role in the Ukrainian health system. Patients wishing to access specialized care free of charge need a referral—provided electronically as an e-referral—from a PHC provider. To access medicines provided at pharmacies through the AMP, they need an e-prescription from a PHC provider. The NHSU monitors PHC providers for contractual compliance and potential fraud, but there is no monitoring of performance or quality, and clinical audits are not conducted. The NHSU intended to introduce contract conditionalities related to performance in 2021, focusing on preventive care, risk group screening, and access to outpatient medicines for target groups of patients with chronic conditions. Starting in September 2021, a top-up performance payment was introduced for the vaccination of children up to age 6 years against measles. Although there is a requirement that care should be compliant with clinical guidelines, Ukraine does not yet have a standardized set of clinical guidelines in place, and providers can follow clinical guidelines of their choice from other countries.

PHC delivery in Ukraine is increasingly embracing digital technology. Beyond e-referrals and e-prescriptions, the use of electronic medical records enables providers to access patient histories and track care provided. It also enables the NHSU to monitor providers and patients for potential fraud and to learn about patterns of behavior that could inform policy making. The law makes provision for telemedicine, and there have been several telemedicine pilots related to PHC provision. The COVID-19 pandemic accelerated the use of digital technologies for consultations, including via social media.

Starting in 2021, the MoH and the NHSU introduced a gradual expansion of the PHC services covered by the PMG. The expansion includes mental and behavioral disorders, additional laboratory tests, COVID-19 vaccination, and services related to the management of patients with chronic diseases and TB. In 2021, the NHSU will also introduce a pay-for-performance top-up to reward attainment of measles vaccination coverage goals, which may set a precedent for future pay-for-performance incentives. What is not yet in place is a clear and comprehensive vision for the expansion of PHC services and the changing role of PHC in the wider health system. The *White Paper on the Health Service Delivery Model in Ukraine,* drafted by the WHO and the MoH, has informed ongoing discussions on PHC and its relationship with hospital services but has not yet been formally adopted. The MoH is also drafting the *Concept of Primary Health Care Development in Ukraine to 2031.*

The Affordable Medicines Program

The AMP—managed by the NSHU since 2019 and previously by SNGs through an earmarked grant from the central government—aims to provide affordable access to outpatient prescription medicines. It covers outpatient medicines for a few priority conditions—mainly cardiovascular diseases, bronchial asthma, and Type 2 diabetes—provided that a prescription is provided by a PHC provider and filled at an NHSU-contracted pharmacy. The NHSU reimburses contracted pharmacies directly for AMP prescriptions, using the e-prescription part of the e-health system.

The list of eligible medicines in the AMP is defined using international nonproprietary names (INNs) and then specified by brands through a call to companies whose medicines are included in the EML. The AMP currently includes 297 medicines, based on 27 INNs. To date, the selection of medicines for inclusion in the AMP, and the EML on which the AMP draws, has not been informed by a clear methodology or updated regularly. However, in December 2020, the CabMin approved the introduction of the Health Technology Assessment (HTA) for the purpose of EML updating (CabMin Resolution 1300), with detailed regulations to be completed in 2021. The use of the HTA promises to improve the clinical appropriateness and efficiency of the AMP.

The MoH sets reimbursement policy using a combination of international and domestic price referencing. Data from five Eastern European countries—the Czech Republic, Hungary, Latvia, Poland, and Slovakia—are used to define a median reference price for each INN. Brand-name generics in the local market that are priced above the reference/international price are not reimbursed. For each reimbursed INN, the cheapest brand-name generic price in the local market becomes the reimbursement reference tariff. Brand-name generics in the local market that are priced below the reimbursement (international) price but above the reimbursement reference tariff (domestic) are reimbursed, but the patient has to pay the difference. Patients can thus obtain the cheapest generic free of charge. This approach to price-setting is considered good practice.

The number of pharmacies contracted and the number of patients covered by the AMP continues to grow. As of March 2021, 9,295 pharmacies or drug-dispensing points operating under 1,136 legal entities had participated in the AMP. National coverage increased from 16.1 to 22.9 pharmacies per 100,000 population between 2019 and 2021, and the number of patients who had used AMP benefits stood at 2.8 million as of March 2021.[7] Equity in access remains a challenge: although all oblasts saw increases in the number of AMP-contracted pharmacies between 2019 and 2021, coverage across oblasts ranged from 17 to 30 pharmacies per 100,000 population (figure 1.5).[8]

Another potential challenge to access is that a fixed monthly budget is set aside for the AMP at the national level, with the monthly spending limit defined based on trends in prescriptions by disease groups. Once that limit is reached, prescriptions eligible for reimbursement are halted until the following month. In practice, this limit has not yet been exceeded.

In 2021, the AMP was expanded to include insulin (starting in July) and 10 additional INNs for mental and neurological disorders (starting in October).[9] The first prescription needs to be provided by a specialist, such as an endocrinologist, psychiatrist, or neurologist; PHC physicians can then write prescriptions for refills.

FIGURE 1.5

Number of pharmacies participating in the AMP per 100,000 people, by oblast, 2019 and 2021

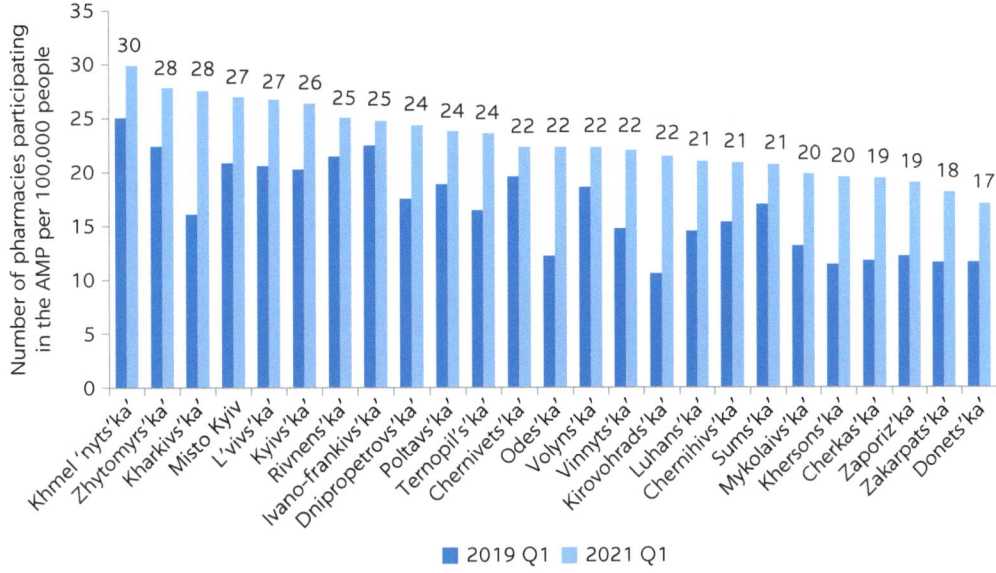

Source: Data from the National Health Service of Ukraine.
Note: AMP = Affordable Medicines Program; Q1 = first quarter.

Specialized outpatient, prehospital emergency, and hospital inpatient care

The PMG for specialized outpatient, prehospital emergency, and hospital inpatient care was introduced at a point when the health care system was still highly hospital-centric. Despite a reduction in hospitalization rates since the hospital right-sizing initiatives of 2015, which brought hospitalization rates for curative care in Ukraine to levels similar to those in its EU13 neighbors, the average length of stay (ALOS) remains substantially higher for Ukraine (10.3 days) than its neighbors (6.6 days).[10] Ukraine also maintains a segregated system of general and disease-specific hospitals, which treat many patients who could potentially be treated on an outpatient basis. For example, 4.1 percent of hospital beds in Ukraine are used to treat TB patients, with an ALOS of 85.6 days in 2019, and a large network of psychiatric hospitals accounts for 11.4 percent of all hospital beds.

Specialized outpatient care is delivered by outpatient units in hospitals, clinical-diagnostic centers (reformed former polyclinics), specialized mono-profile outpatient clinics, and private solo practices. There is not yet sufficient coordination between PHC and specialized outpatient care or adequately comprehensive attempts to shift ambulatory-sensitive conditions out of the hospital setting, although some progress has been made on mental health. The new e-referral system provides an opportunity to analyze the flow of different types of referrals and improve the right-sizing of care.

In early 2020, the government approved a list of 212 "hub hospitals" to constitute the network of providers—the "Capable Network"—to be developed in the future. The move represents an important step toward a more rational and efficient approach to investment in the hospital sector, but care needs to be taken to ensure that the list of hospitals is optimal. Still lacking is an approved formal strategy that lays out the vision for an integrated model of service delivery across all types of care, potentially building on the (draft) *White Paper on Health Service Delivery Model in Ukraine.*

Specialized care services within the PMG are divided into service packages, each contracted separately with providers. As of 2020, there were 29 specialized care packages. They include four COVID-19 packages for testing by mobile brigades, prehospital emergency care, hospitalization, and a COVID–related salary top-up, which were added in response to the pandemic. Sixteen packages relate to medical conditions, such as acute stroke, childbirth, mental health, TB, HIV, and COVID-19; they cover a comprehensive set of services to treat them. Nine packages are defined as service inputs (colonoscopy, hemodialysis, radiotherapy), which can be used to treat a variety of conditions. Four packages are broadly defined by the provider setting—inpatient surgical, inpatient nonsurgical, outpatient, and emergency care—to cover all care that does not fall into the other groups. All specialized care packages in the PMG except outpatient care explicitly cover medicines. In practice, many medicines are purchased out-of-pocket by inpatients. In 2020, a new referral requirement was adopted, to improve the integration of specialized care and primary care within the PMG. In order to receive specialized treatment free of charge, the patient requires an electronic referral from a primary care or other specialized care provider. Contracting is optional; providers can pick and choose which packages to apply. This system exacerbates existing inefficiencies, as providers apply only for packages that are most economically attractive. It also contributes to geographic inequities in access to care.

To be contracted by the NHSU, providers must meet a range of service delivery requirements. They include universal requirements, including those related to legal status, licensing, and e-health functionalities; package-specific requirements, related to facility characteristics, medical personnel, and equipment; and additional relevant licenses (for nuclear medicine or narcotics, for example). Services provided outside the contracted packages are not necessarily reported. Contracted facilities are required to be legally autonomous from the state, to create a purchaser/provider split, and to remove potential conflicts of interest. As part of the reform, hospitals may also open bank accounts at commercial banks rather than the Treasury. This new autonomy requires new governance and accountability arrangements, and new regulations are needed to strengthen it. Between April and December 2020, the NHSU contracted and made payments to 1,681 specialized providers, including 59 private facilities and 25 oblast-level emergency medical care centers for its specialized care packages.

In 2020, most of the specialized care in the PMG—81 percent of specialized care and 67 percent of the total PMG budget—was purchased using global budgets. These purchases included all emergency care, all surgical care, all nonsurgical hospital care not paid for using DRG–based payments, and select procedures that are by fee-for-service (figure 1.6). For each PMG package contracted on a global budget, the NHSU has defined a "base rate" per service unit, which is adjusted to account for variation in service costs. For example, the outpatient base rate is multiplied by 9.713 for surgical procedures and 0.186 for a dental care intervention and then multiplied by the number services that the contractor provided the previous year to obtain the global budget paid to each contracted facility. A global budget is also used for the new COVID-19 packages, because of the lack of predictability of case numbers.

FIGURE 1.6

Provider payment arrangements for the PMG in the second and third quarters of 2020

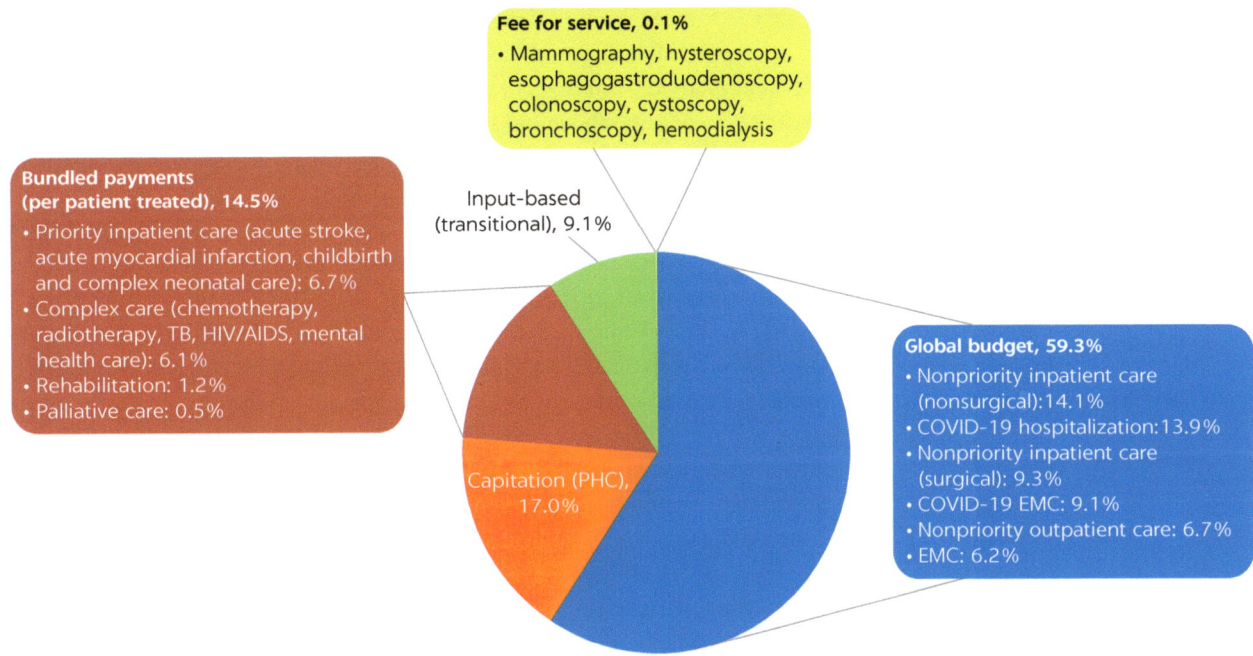

Fee for service, 0.1%
• Mammography, hysteroscopy, esophagogastroduodenoscopy, colonoscopy, cystoscopy, bronchoscopy, hemodialysis

Bundled payments (per patient treated), 14.5%
• Priority inpatient care (acute stroke, acute myocardial infarction, childbirth and complex neonatal care): 6.7%
• Complex care (chemotherapy, radiotherapy, TB, HIV/AIDS, mental health care): 6.1%
• Rehabilitation: 1.2%
• Palliative care: 0.5%

Input-based (transitional), 9.1%

Capitation (PHC), 17.0%

Global budget, 59.3%
• Nonpriority inpatient care (nonsurgical):14.1%
• COVID-19 hospitalization:13.9%
• Nonpriority inpatient care (surgical): 9.3%
• COVID-19 EMC: 9.1%
• Nonpriority outpatient care: 6.7%
• EMC: 6.2%

Source: National Health Service of Ukraine dashboard.
Note: COVID-19 = coronavirus (pandemic). EMC = emergency medical care; PHC = primary health care; TB = tuberculosis.

Since April 2020, case-based payments have been used for four inpatient conditions: acute stroke (one case for all types), acute myocardial infarction, childbirth (one case for all types), and complex neonatal care. Bottom-up costing was used to ensure that these rates cover the full cost of care. Together, these four conditions account for 8.1 percent of all specialized care contracts. Fee-for-service payments are used for seven outpatient services—including endoscopy, mammography, and hemodialysis—to incentivize provision and investment in equipment for these services. Fee-for-service payments accounted for only 0.1 percent of specialized care in the PMG in 2020.

The MoH and the NHSU had intended to gradually introduce more DRG–based payments for hospitals, starting in May 2020; these efforts were postponed because of the COVID-19 pandemic . The original plan was to split hospital payment into a global budget and a case-based amount, with the case-based amount gradually increasing from 10 percent to 40 percent by July 2020. In parallel, providers would be required to start coding and reporting their cases using the Ukrainian DRGs (UDRGs), which are based on the Australian Refined DRGs (AR-DRGs) but are aggregated into a larger number of groups (131, in addition to the 4 case-based payments).

The introduction of DRGs was initially postponed from May until June; in June it was postponed until October; in September it was canceled for 2020. The decision was made for several reasons. First, the UDRG grouping of 131 categories was evaluated as excessively broad, leaving a high degree of cost heterogeneity within individual groups, thereby creating considerable financial risk for providers. Second, these financial risks would be exacerbated by the COVID-19 pandemic, which was expected to depress the use of essential services and, therefore, hospital revenues. Instead, payment for specialized care was based on the historical number of services provided, recalculated using the average tariff to determine the amount to be reimbursed. Thus, in 2020, the NHSU exclusively used global budgets and fee-for-service as the payment method for hospital care, with the exception of the four case-based packages mentioned above and some COVID–related top-ups described below. Although hospitals did not transition to DRG payments in 2020, hospitals started reporting cases using DRGs in June 2020.

In 2020, the government provided select hospitals with two forms of substantial additional financial support to offset potential losses associated with the health financing reform and COVID-19. In June 2020, the government introduced transitional lump-sum top-ups to ensure that providers do not bear excessive losses as a result of the payment reform, raising their budgets to at least 90 percent of the amount they had historically received through central government grants. These payments were made to 519 communal facilities and amounted to 1.6 percent of the 2020 PMG contract value of UAH 2.1 billion. In September 2020, the government provided additional subsidies to SNGs to increase the salaries of medical staff who treated COVID-19 cases, to compensate them for the additional workload and risk. In addition, starting in September 2020, salary increases of 30–70 percent over base salaries were provided to all medical personnel except those working in primary care via NHSU contracts.[11] These measures were extended through the end of the first quarter of 2021 and then discontinued in April 2021. Together, these two top-ups amounted to 9.1 percent of 2020 PMG spending.

Recommendations for improving the purchasing of PMG services

Primary health care

The PHC component of the health financing reform is well designed and is being implemented effectively. Some actions that could further improve it include the following:

- Articulate and approve a long-term strategic vision for PHC, with a clearly defined service delivery model that is responsive to people's needs, and align purchasing arrangements to support this vision.
- Introduce standardized clinical protocols and mandate them for use within the PMG at the PHC level, starting with priority conditions (such as major noncommunicable diseases). Doing so would not only help ensure clinical care quality but also guide providers on the most cost-effective care they can provide within their capitation budget.
- Accelerate the use of digital technologies in health care delivery, from further development of the e-health architecture to implementation of telemedicine, supported by a strategy and action plan that will ensure the appropriate investment, regulations, and skills.
- Introduce a performance monitoring framework for PHC to measure performance across and within facilities over time, and improve accountability for the delivery of quality care.

The Affordable Medicines Program

The AMP is playing an important role in providing the population with free or low-cost medicines for conditions that affect a large share of the population and can be effectively managed. The following measures could improve its clinical appropriateness, cost-effectiveness, and equity:

- Update the EML, on which the AMP draws, to ensure that the medicines included are aligned with modern clinical guidelines and cost-effective. To ensure timely updates of the EML, finalize the regulations governing the new HTA process (which will be used to update the EML), per the schedule established by the December 2020 CabMin Resolution.
- Assess the trade-offs between including more conditions and medicines in the AMP and ensuring sufficient funding for less costly, cost-effective medicines that treat conditions that affect a large number of people (with the latter a priority). The HTA can also play a role in this effort.
- Ensure that as the AMP expands, it does so equitably across regions and socioeconomic areas within each region, in order to reduce geographic imbalances in population access to AMP–contracted pharmacies. The NHSU and the MoH could approach pharmacies in underserved areas for potential contracting.
- Explore the potential for the NHSU to play a role in monitoring prescribing behavior, through the e-prescription system and the recently strengthened e-health system. Doing so would enable the NHSU to identify potential fraud by providers or patients and improve the clinical quality of care, by assessing whether prescriptions are needed and suitable for the diagnosed condition.

Specialized outpatient, prehospital emergency, and hospital care

The specialized care component of the PMG is where most policy attention is needed—understandably, as contracting for these services began only last year, in the midst of the COVID-19 pandemic. Policy needs to ensure access to care and efficiency while managing the financial risk of patients and providers. Recommendations for improving this component include the following:

- Refine the grouping of PMG service packages and the UDRGs intended to pay for them by (a) unbundling the broadly defined packages—outpatient, inpatient surgical, inpatient nonsurgical, and emergency care packages—into more explicitly defined packages of care and specifying more clearly the remaining services in the four packages; (b) regrouping packages that represent inputs into other services (for example, chemotherapy and radiotherapy) as part of packages to treat specific conditions (such as breast cancer); and (c) further unbundling the UDRGs, as the original 131 groups are not clinically similar or cost-homogeneous enough, leading to significant cost variation across cases and possible financial risk.
- Lay out a clear transition pathway toward DRG payments that provides facilities with protection against excessive financial risk and gives facilities time to adjust (to develop their coding capacities and adjusting clinical practice, for example). Options include creating risk corridors, paying partially by DRG and partially by global budget, and providing feedback to providers on how to improve service delivery for greater efficiency and deal with unexpected threats, such as the COVID-19 pandemic.
- Replace selective contracting of providers, in which providers get to choose which packages they want to deliver, with comprehensive contracts that guarantee patients equitable access to all service packages in the PMG.

Providers in the Capable Network should be required to provide all services appropriate to their level. Signing multiyear, rather than annual, contracts would give providers the incentive to invest in the inputs needed to provide new services.

- Review the Capable Network Plan to ensure a more transparent hospital selection methodology in which inclusion criteria are aligned with policy principles, such as ensuring sufficient service volumes, avoiding fragmentation, and ensuring equity of geographic access.
- Continue to strengthen use of NHSU data for decision-making. These data can be used not only to identify miscoding, upcoding, and abuse by providers or patients but also to support policy decisions within the health sector on issues such as selection of hub hospitals for the Capable Network, the optimization of care pathways, the content of benefit packages, and the evaluation of the effects of provider payment reform.

GOVERNANCE ARRANGEMENTS FOR THE PMG

The creation of a health service purchasing agency such as the NHSU, along with the introduction into the health system of the strategic purchasing function, requires changes in governance structures. The key functions of these governance structures should be to set the strategic direction for the purchasing agency and to hold it accountable for resource use and results. Five aspects of governance are essential: the autonomy of the purchasing agency, clarity in roles and methodologies, effective interagency coordination, external accountability, and internal control. Adequate capacity of all agencies involved in governance arrangements, especially the NHSU and the MoH, in terms of personnel and other resources is also critical. This chapter provides a detailed discussion of governance arrangements for the PMG.

The NHSU is autonomous in law, but to ensure that it can effectively function as an autonomous purchasing agency, the NHSU, the MoH, and the MoF all need to further adapt to their new institutional roles. The NHSU was established as a Central Executive Agency. This means that it has autonomy in technical and operational matters but not policy decisions, which the government makes. The MoH remains responsible for overall health sector policies. The MoF is responsible for fiscal policy, which affects the NHSU budget allocation; under the law, it also has a joint role, with the MoH, in approving major policy decisions that affect the NHSU's budget. This new arrangement somewhat modifies the traditional institutional roles of the MoH and the MoF, which need to transition to arms' length stewardship of the NHSU without getting involved in technical and operational matters. The NHSU needs to fully assume the role of an implementing agency that provides neutral technical advice and faithfully implements the political choices made by the government. As in other countries, agencies may take time to adapt to their new roles. Frequent dialogue between the leadership of the three entities and strengthening of the capacity of their staff can accelerate adaptation.

For all entities to function and cooperate effectively under the new arrangement, their roles and related processes need to be better defined. The law defines the overall institutional architecture of the new system and the roles of the CabMin, the MoH, the MoF, and the NHSU in decision-making related to the PMG, but regulatory gaps persist pertaining to the rules for defining and financing the PMG. In particular, there is no systematic methodology for establishing PMG priorities or designing the benefit package, weighing the costs and benefits of services, or determining the contract specifications to be used by the NHSU. These processes need to be transparent, evidence-informed, and mindful of NHSU budget constraints. They also need to incorporate a medium-term perspective in planning and priority-setting, coordinated with the budget cycle. It is also important to develop a clear framework for consultations with the general public and the medical community on issues related to the PMG, which would strengthen transparency and lend legitimacy to the choices the government makes.

Interagency cooperation would benefit from stronger planning and more constructive transitions after changes of leadership. Coordination and cooperation by the NHSU, the MoH, the MoF, and the CabMin is also critical to strategic health purchasing. Good processes for meetings, decisions, and communications are needed, as well as a shared strategic plan and policy frameworks to guide the contributions of the MoH, the NHSU, health care providers, and SNGs. The Ukrainian health sector lacks a strategic plan developed and agreed to by the MoH, the NHSU, and key health sector stakeholders that is aligned with a multiyear health financing strategy and endorsed by the government. A strategic vision would help accelerate the process of building constructive relationships across agencies after transitions of the government or ministers. Transitions, which are frequent in Ukraine, are often challenging. Conflict and lack of alignment between the NHSU and the MoH can inappropriately push the responsibility for health sector stewardship onto the MoF; lack of cooperation between the MoH and the MoF may weaken their roles in strategic stewardship and NHSU governance.

Successful interagency cooperation also requires better alignment between central and subnational levels, especially in policies related to rationalizing the facility network. A significant share of financing still flows through subnational budgets, and SNGs are responsible for developing and maintaining their network of health facilities, in compliance with the contractual requirements of the NHSU. In particular, SNGs are responsible for the deficits and debts of their facilities and have the option of bailing out ineffective and loss-making health care providers. Although this mechanism is useful for coping during a health financing transition and the COVID-19 crisis, it creates risks for system efficiency and accountability. In the medium and longer terms, the NHSU and the MoH will need to strengthen their coordination with SNGs and hospital districts to rationalize the facility network and make it more efficient. These measures should also include stronger accountability of the newly autonomous health care facilities, in terms of both contractual accountability to the NHSU and accountability to their owners, the SNGs.

A critical governance requirement is for the NHSU, as the newly created strategic purchaser, to be accountable to the CabMin, the government's audit authorities, and the Public Control Council (PPC). External accountability is central to building trust in the NHSU as a capable purchaser, as well as in the health reform in general. As a Central Executive Agency, the NHSU reports via the MoH to the CabMin, with the MoH and the MoF having joint authority over key policy decisions governing health financing and NHSU purchasing, including approval of the PMG, tariffs, and budget proposals. Lack of an effective forum for the MoH and the MoF to engage with each other on health financing impedes development of a shared strategic vision and effective oversight of the NHSU. This issue could be addressed by creating an NHSU oversight committee involving the MoH and the MoF, perhaps chaired by a representative of the Prime Minister's Office. Ideally, the NHSU also needs to have a set of annual and medium-term performance objectives, which would become the basis of its accountability to the government. The NHSU is responsive to recommendations from the mandatory audits by the State Audit Authority, the National Anti-Corruption Committee, and the Accounting Chamber of Ukraine, but not all reports are publicly available; it would be good practice to publish all of them. The NHSU also reports to the Public Control Council (PCC), which is made up of patients and civil society members. The PCC's role is only advisory, however; it does not have the governance powers or responsibilities of a supervisory board. Accountability could be strengthened by providing formal oversight of the PCC by the MoH and CabMin and better defining its role.

In addition to external accountability, the NHSU needs an impeccable system of internal control to ensure that it extracts the best value from its resources and does not tolerate fraud. The NHSU is responsible for ensuring spending discipline by preventing breaches of the budget and the inappropriate use of resources by the NHSU or the facilities it contracts. Managing its responsibility within its approved budget requires that the NHSU use appropriate data and methods in forecasting demand, costing the PMG, and formulating its budget proposal and that the government (on the advice of the MoF and the MoH) ensures that the approved budget is realistic. The NHSU developed, and continues to strengthen, internal control measures to prevent mistakes and fraud in claims. These measures include independent checks and balances, an operational internal audit unit, and an antifraud program that uses automated monitoring based on algorithms to detect potentially fraudulent claims. The automated monitoring is supposed to be followed up by monitoring visits to investigate cases; the frequency of these visits should be increased. Doing so requires strengthening the NHSU's five subnational offices, as well as adopting and implementing draft by-laws (already prepared) to create the basis for imposing sanctions and penalties on providers. It would also be good practice for the NHSU executive to develop a risk register documenting strategic, financial, operational, and reputational risks and corresponding risk management measures, which the internal audit unit would regularly review.

To successfully assume the complex new role of strategic purchaser, the NHSU needs to become a highly capable organization, with stronger staffing and IT capacities. Its level of staffing (266 central and 53 subnational staff in February 2021) and the size of its administrative budget relative to its program budget for purchasing services (0.23 percent) are lean, constraining the full development of its strategic purchasing function. Issues that need to be addressed include the shortage of analytical staff at the NHSU, particularly its five subnational offices, and the MoH; a shortage that is driven in part by low salaries in segments such as IT. The MoH should consider (i) increasing NHSU staff numbers within the total limit already approved, with flexibility to reallocate posts between central and subnational offices, and (ii) developing the analytical skills of NHSU staff to support the development of strategic purchasing. In addition to human resources, the NHSU needs to significantly expand and enhance its IT systems. It relies on external funding from development partners for most of its software and lacks resources for upgrades and licenses. In the medium term, as the e-health system for health care providers is developed further, it will be important to invest in the coordinated development of the NHSU's IT and data management systems, to ensure integration with the wider e-health system and avoid duplicative systems.

Recommendations for improving the governance of the PMG include the following:

- Create a CabMin committee to act as an oversight committee for the NHSU, and facilitate better interagency coordination by the MoF, the MoH, the NHSU, and other ministries in setting the strategic directions for the NHSU and reaching consensus on issues such as health financing strategy and PMG budget and tariffs.
- As part of Ukraine's new developments in performance-based oversight of policy implementation by the CabMin, consider piloting a mechanism through which the MoH would facilitate the NHSU's accountability to the CabMin for relevant aspects of the sector policy implementation, clearly defining responsibilities for agreeing on and reviewing performance objectives.
- Develop an NHSU organizational strategy that is aligned with the health financing strategy and with the performance objectives and indicators proposed above by which the NHSU can be held accountable to the CabMin.
- Establish a small permanent unit in the MoH with technical expertise in health financing policy, to enable the MoH to better perform its stewardship and governance roles with respect to the NHSU, including its roles on the CabMin committee overseeing the NHSU.
- Further specify the role and procedures of the PCC with respect to NHSU governance in a CabMin order, including the information and reports the NHSU should provide to the PCC, and formalize a mechanism by which the PCC can share its findings and recommendations with the MoH and the CabMin committee proposed above.

NOTES

1. Still excluded from the PMG are highly specialized and experimental procedures, which are provided mainly by facilities reporting to Ukraine's National Academy of Medical Sciences rather than the MoH and which might be considered "quaternary care." It is envisaged that all of these advanced services will eventually be absorbed by the PMG, which currently covers up to tertiary care. The legal mandate of the PMG covers tertiary care; it does not delineate quaternary care from tertiary care.
2. The European region in this report refers to the WHO European region. It includes Albania, Andorra, Armenia, Austria, Azerbaijan, Belarus, Belgium, Bosnia and Herzegovina, Bulgaria, Croatia, Cyprus, the Czech Republic, Denmark, Estonia, Finland, France, Georgia, Germany, Greece, Hungary, Iceland, Ireland, Israel, Italy, Kazakhstan, the Kyrgyz Republic, Latvia, Lithuania, Luxembourg, Malta, Moldova, Monaco, Montenegro, the Netherlands, North Macedonia, Norway, Poland, Portugal, Romania, the Russian Federation, San Marino, Serbia, the Slovak Republic, Slovenia, Spain, Sweden, Switzerland, Tajikistan, Turkey, Turkmenistan, Ukraine, the United Kingdom, and Uzbekistan.
3. Out-of-pocket payments greater than 10 percent of total household consumption is the global metric used to monitor catastrophic health spending as part of Sustainable Development Goal (SDG) 3.8 on Universal Health Coverage. Member States in the WHO European Region also monitor catastrophic spending using a "capacity to pay" approach, which is more sensitive to financial hardship among poorer households than the SDG approach. Capacity to pay for health care is country specific and measured as a household's total consumption minus a standard amount to cover basic needs, such as food, housing, and utilities.
4. Total debt repayment needs in 2021 alone are projected to be 10 percent of GDP.
5. Subnational budget plans for 2021 were not yet approved at the time of writing, so the consolidated health spending figure was not available.

6. Government spending on health in Ukraine now meets the minimum (12 percent) that WHO Europe recommends to its Member States.

7. Despite the increase in the number of patients, the number of prescriptions dropped significantly during the COVID-19 pandemic. In November 2020, for example, the number of prescriptions was down by almost a quarter year-on-year, according to data from the NHSU.

8. Figures were calculated using the NHSU dashboard (for data on number of pharmacies) and the State Statistics Service of Ukraine (for data on population).

9. See https://zakon.rada.gov.ua/laws/show/133-2021-%D0%BF#Text.

10. Ukraine data are for 2019 (MoH Center of Medical Statistics); EU13 data are for 2018 (https://stats.oecd.org/).

11. The value of the top-ups to existing NHSU contracts through the PMG was calculated based on actual personnel numbers. The salary increases were 70 percent for doctors, 50 percent for nurses, and 30 percent for junior medical staff.

2 Funding the Program of Medical Guarantees

WHAT IS THE PROGRAM OF MEDICAL GUARANTEES?

The Program of Medical Guarantees (PMG) specifies the national health care benefit package and is funded through a single program in the central budget. Before the 2017 health financing reform, most of the medical services in Ukraine were funded through subnational governments (SNGs), which received earmarked health grants from the central budget and supplemented those amounts with local revenue. In this way, the centrally collected general taxes, such as the value-added tax (VAT), were allocated to around 800 regional and local budgets for oblasts, rayons, cities, and hromadas,[1] creating a high degree of fragmentation. The core innovation of the reform was to pool most government health spending under a single central program executed by the national purchaser, the National Health Service of Ukraine (NHSU). This program covers purchases of medical services included in the PMG. The 2017 law defines the PMG as the description of medical goods and services fully funded by the state, so it is commonly understood as the specification of the national health care benefit package. At the same time, the PMG is also a program within the state budget that pays for most of the procurement of these services and goods. A portion of the PMG continues to be supplemented by SNGs through smaller local programs.

Although the reform has shifted most of the responsibility for PMG financing to the central government, SNGs are still expected to fund the cost of utilities out of local revenue. The NHSU purchases PMG services based on tariffs, which do not assume an explicit breakdown by cost components such as capitation, case rates, and global budgets. This represents a departure from the previous funding system, where facility budgets were approved and funded strictly by economic classification lines based on respective spending norms. At the same time, the law requires SNGs, as facility owners, to pay for the utility costs of the services in the PMG. This rule was introduced as a temporary measure against the backdrop of significant fiscal pressures on the central government following the 2014–15 economic crisis on the assumption that the NHSU rates were, in that context, insufficient to cover utility costs. Whether the rates were indeed insufficient remained a matter of judgment because the PMG costing methodology was not explicit in these first years. At the primary health care (PHC) level, capitation payments introduced in 2018 were assessed to cover all recurrent costs, including utilities, and even provided some space for small capital investment, depending on the chosen organization of service provision. As a result, assigning specific cost components to the SNGs while keeping the NHSU rates deliberately broad in economic component coverage created risks of duplicating or underfunding services.

The SNGs also retain the right to supplement the current costs borne by the PMG. By introducing the PMG, the government pooled the responsibility for most of the curative health care financing at the central government level. However, in addition to the responsibility for utility cost coverage, the new arrangement allowed the SNGs to supplement other current costs of the PMG providers with local revenue. In this way, the SNGs received an opportunity to subsidize loss-making communal facilities, covering their deficits and debts.

The PMG is funded by the NHSU within a budget constraint voted by the Parliament, but this constraint is softened by the overlap in the assignment of financing responsibility with the SNGs. The annual allocation to the PMG is approved within the program-based budget law. The Parliament votes for the overall program allocation without disaggregating by individual components, and this overall program limit cannot change without amendments to the budget law.[2] However, SNG supplementation of the PMG funding creates an overlap between the central and subnational financing assignment. On the one hand, this overlap makes it possible for the SNGs as the owners of local hospitals to cover their deficits and motivates the SNGs to address inefficiencies in hospital service delivery. On the other hand, the possibility for the SNGs to bail out inefficient hospitals is a potential barrier to achieving efficiency gains through the hard budget constraint that would be imposed if there were only a central government allocation.

Services already included in the PMG and those to be transferred into the PMG in the future account for at least three-fourths of government-consolidated health expenditures, with the rest going to preventive health, administration, and research. The PMG was launched in 2018, initially covering only PHC services. On April 1, 2020, it was expanded to include specialized and emergency care as well as the Affordable Medicines Program (AMP), which pays for outpatient medicines. In 2020, this expanded benefit package is estimated to have consumed 68 percent of overall consolidated health spending. As illustrated in figure 2.1, this amount included 53 percent spent on the PMG by the NHSU and 9 percent spent by the SNGs to fund specialized and emergency care during the first quarter when it was not yet pooled under the PMG and was financed through a health grant. It also included 6 percent paid by the SNGs to directly cover utility costs associated with the PMG; although utility payments are not pooled through the NHSU, they represent expenditures on services included in the PMG package. Moreover, the reform assumes that a range of highly specialized curative services currently funded through the Ministry of Health (MoH) and other central agencies would be ultimately absorbed by the PMG; their approximate cost in 2020 was around 5 percent of consolidated government health spending. Combined, all these PMG and proxy-PMG services take up 73 percent of consolidated health spending. This does not include capital costs, which are paid by the local governments that own facilities supplying PMG services—around 6 percent of consolidated health spending—and MoH investment in the highly specialized public hospitals reporting to the ministry.

FIGURE 2.1
Consolidated health spending—2020 plan, June 2020

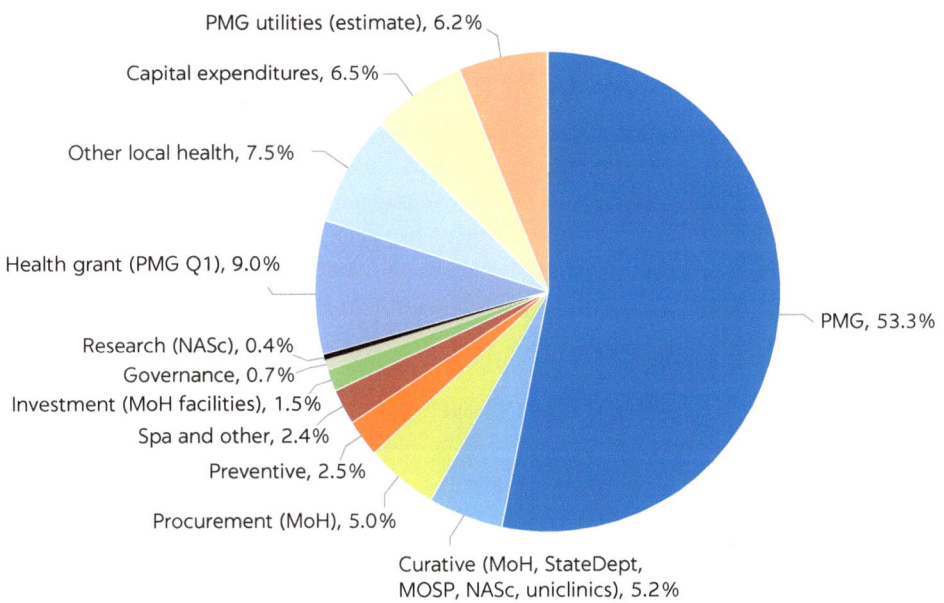

Source: State Treasury Service of Ukraine.
Note: MoH = Ministry of Health; MoSP = Ministry of Social Policy; NASc = National Academy of Sciences; PMG = Program of Medical Guarantees; Spa = facilities providing spa services, which include a medical component to support treatment and rehabilitation of the patients.

Rather than introducing new services, the PMG reflects the articulation and concentration of the broad commitment to providing health care that is free at the point of use into a more explicit benefit package. Ukraine's Constitution contains an open commitment of the state to "organize and fund health care services to ensure the right of every person to protection of their health" and ensure that public facilities provide health care services free of charge. The PMG transforms this open-ended commitment into a more explicit service package that can be guaranteed to the population through state-funded schemes. The law requires the PMG to cover the entire care continuum—primary, specialized, emergency, rehabilitation, and palliative care—but based on a quantifiable list of services to be purchased at an agreed-on price.

By the 2017 law, the PMG covers all Ukrainian citizens, permanent residents, and refugees[3] and is therefore essentially exhaustive in its population coverage. In parallel to the health budget spent on the PMG, Ukraine continues to separately fund medical care for military and civil security personnel as well as medical services provided within the penitentiary system and residential social service institutions. These expenditures are included in the budgets of other sectors, are not classified as health care, and are not easily traceable. The new Military Medicine Doctrine, approved in 2018, intends to integrate military health care into what it calls "Ukraine's single medical space" but without providing a clear definition of this term, including whether military health care would be incorporated into the general government health care budget and potentially paid through the PMG. The government also still needs to develop its vision for coordinating the PMG with medical expenditures in the social sector.

THE ROLE OF PRIVATE, OUT-OF-POCKET SPENDING

Ukraine has a remarkably high level of out-of-pocket (OOP) health care spending, which, as a share of current health spending, has been rapidly increasing. In 2018, OOP spending generated 49.3 percent of the country's current health expenditures.[4] This is much higher than the 38.4 percent average for lower-middle-income countries (LMICs), although it is similar to the 50.6 percent average for LMICs in the European Region (figure 2.2) and substantially up from its 38 percent share in 2005.[5] In absolute terms, OOP spending has grown rapidly over the past decade, from 2.3 percent of gross domestic product (GDP) in 2005 to 3.7 percent of GDP in 2018, while government health spending has remained almost unchanged, at 3.7 percent of GDP throughout the same period. Private pooled spending is not an important source of health financing in Ukraine because private health insurance is not widespread; in 2018, it funded around 0.9 percent of the total current health expenditures.[6]

OOP spending in Ukraine is highly concentrated in payments for medicines and medical goods. Within total OOP expenses, 74.9 percent is spent on over-the-counter purchases of medicines and medical goods, based on the 2018 National Health Accounts (NHA), with some of these purchases later used by these patients during inpatient care. It is impossible to identify the exact percentage of privately purchased medicines used in inpatient care from the existing official surveys. There is also no equivalent of the Health Utilization and

FIGURE 2.2

Out-of-pocket spending as a share of current health spending, 2000–18

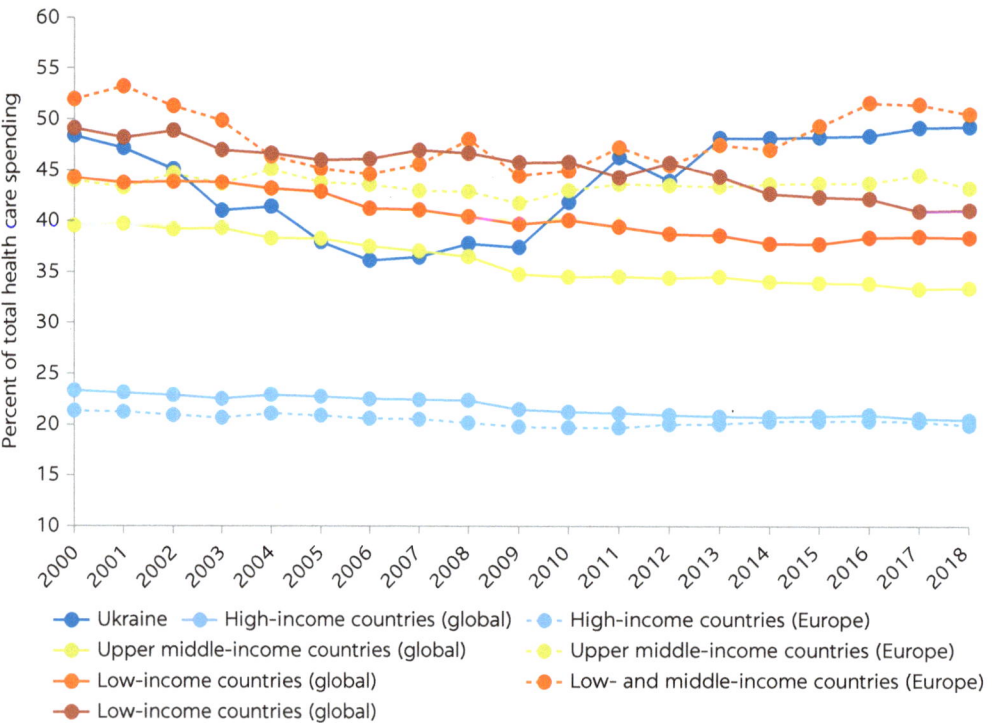

Sources: State Statistics Service of Ukraine (for Ukraine); World Development Indicators database; Global Health Expenditure Database (https://apps.who.int/nha/database).
Note: Regional averages are not population-weighted.

Expenditure Survey (HUES) in Ukraine that would identify which particular types of conditions are associated with the highest level of private spending on medicines, indicating a potential gap in government funding of the respective type of care. However, the survey for the Ukraine Health Index 2019 indicates that within the total number of prescribed medicines—that is, purchases resulting from visiting a medical professional either in an outpatient or in an inpatient setting—about 38.8 percent is used in outpatient care, and 61.2 percent is used in hospitals. It is unclear what share of all purchases is bought without attending medical care facilities and receiving medical advice (self-treatment).

While the share of the consolidated government health budget[7] spent on medicines seems broadly comparable to Organisation for Economic Co-operation and Development (OECD) countries, Ukraine spends a much smaller share of this budget on funding prescribed medicines. In 2015, the latest year for which duly disaggregated data are available, medicines, appliances, and other medical goods[8] constituted 17.9 percent of government-consolidated current health spending (see figure 2.3). In particular, 8.4 percent of consolidated current health care spending was on medical goods used in hospitals and 0.8 percent in polyclinics. Additionally, 8.6 percent of health expenditures in the consolidated budget used for medical goods was spent through centralized procurement.

At that time, the AMP had not yet been launched, and government financing of prescribed medicines to be consumed following the health contact rather than in the process of receiving inpatient or outpatient care was nearly nonexistent. In OECD countries, the share of total current health spending by governments or compulsory schemes on medicines in 2015 (latest available year) ranged from 7.6 percent in Denmark to 16.9 percent in Spain.[9] Assuming that a significant part of Ukraine's reported government expenditures on medical goods was spent on medicines, the overall share of the budget spent on financing medicines in Ukraine seems broadly comparable

FIGURE 2.3
Spending on medical goods—medicines, appliances, and other medical goods—within total current spending on health in the consolidated budget for Ukraine, 2015

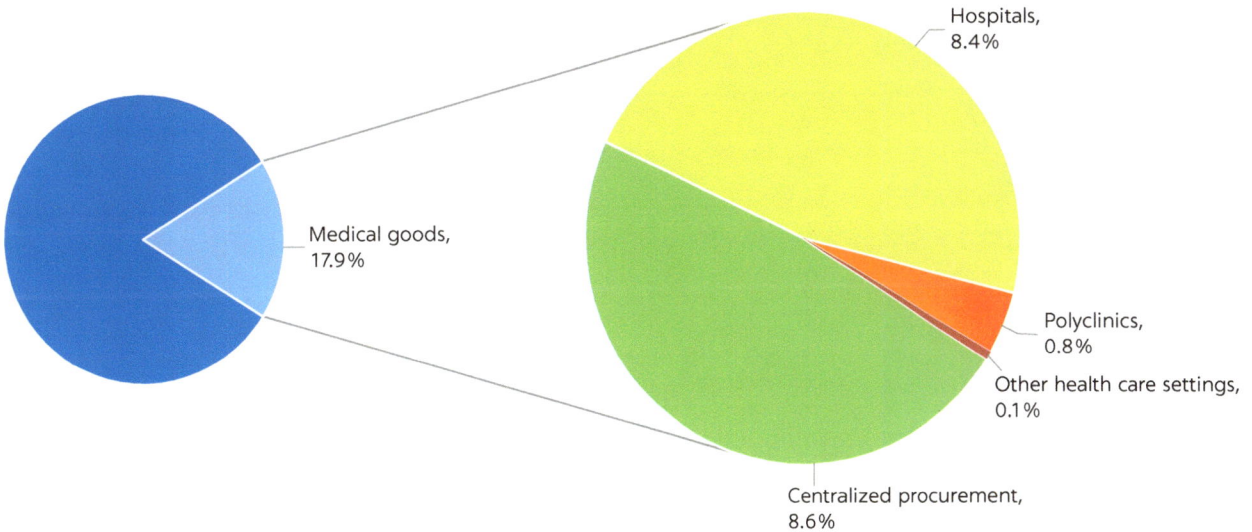

Source: 2015 World Bank BOOST database.

to that of its European neighbors. However, spending on prescribed medicines in these comparator countries ranges from 2.5 percent of current health spending in Denmark to 10.2 percent in Spain. In contrast, these expenditures are much lower in Ukraine, even with the introduction of the AMP (which equaled 0.9 percent of total current consolidated health spending in 2018). As a result, Ukrainians pay for most of their outpatient medicines OOP; in 2018, the share of household financing of medical goods was 99.8 percent.[10] This means that the potential extension of the AMP as a PMG component would be critical for protecting the population from OOP expenses.

Lack of affordability of medicines and tests explains the growing level of self-reported, unmet health care needs, especially in the poorest decile. Unmet needs for medical services in Ukraine are reported by around 24.5 percent of all households (2017–18 average[11]).[12] This percentage of unmet health needs has grown by 1.4 times since 2009 and is most critical in medicines (82 percent of all households with self-reported, unmet health care needs have forgone buying medicines) and diagnostic tests (54 percent of all households with self-reported, unmet needs have forgone diagnostic tests). The key reason for forgoing medical services is cost, especially among rural residents. The sharpest increase in unmet health care needs during 2009–18 was registered in the poorest population decile and the three richest population deciles. Because of the relatively higher growth of the unmet need among the richest groups, the socioeconomic inequality in the reported unmet need for medical services decreased during 2009–18, as illustrated in figure 2.4. The concentration index,[13] which measures the deviation of unmet need income distribution from the full equality line, changed from −0.15 to −0.12 during these years.[14]

FIGURE 2.4

Socioeconomic inequality in the self-reported unmet need for medical services: Changes in the concentration index between 2009 and 2018

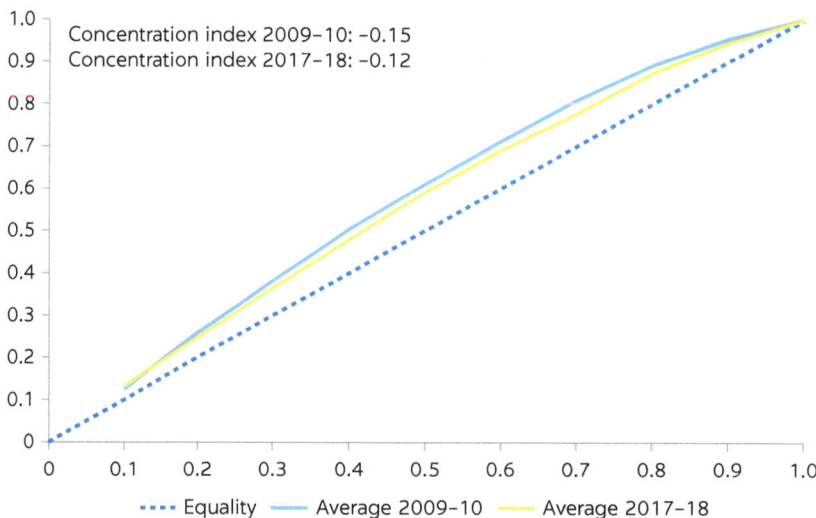

Source: Calculations are based on data collected by the State Statistics Service of Ukraine through the 2009–18 Household Living Condition Survey's module on self-perceived health status.
Note: Incidence of self-reported unmet need for medical services in this figure is measured as a percentage of households reporting an unmet health care need in the total number of households in the relevant category.

FIGURE 2.5

Breakdown of out-of-pocket payments, by type of health care and the consumption quintile, 2019

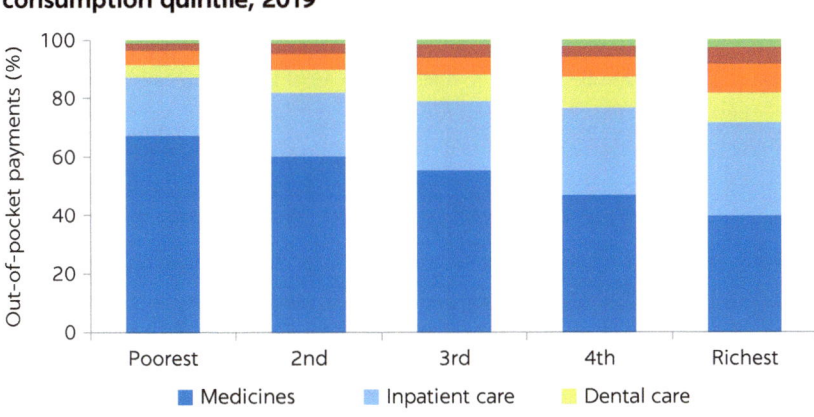

Source: WHO Regional Office for Europe (in press), based on the household budget survey data from the State Statistics Office.

The incidence of catastrophic spending has been increasing in Ukraine over the last decade—a finding that is robust to different measurement approaches. Between 2010 and 2019, the share of the population spending more than 10 percent of their consumption on health care grew from 6.9 percent to 7.8 percent, while the share of households whose health care spending exceeded a normative threshold developed and used by the World Health Organization (WHO)/Europe increased from 11.5 percent to 16.7 percent.[15] Analysis finds that catastrophic spending is heavily concentrated in the poorest consumption quintile.

THE PROCESS OF PMG BENEFIT PACKAGE DEVELOPMENT, COSTING, AND BUDGETING

All health systems ration health service entitlement because of budget constraints, but they differ greatly in how explicitly these choices are made. If rationing is implicit, the decisions about who gets excluded or which services are not covered are made based on hidden rules defined by the providers at the point of care. This leads to OOP expenses or service denial. Alternatively, explicit rationing assumes that choices as to which services are not covered or which individuals are excluded are made openly and systematically, based on transparently discussed priorities, formalized cost-sharing, and specification of the entitlement within a guaranteed benefit package.

With the 2017 health reform, Ukraine moved from a system where services were rationed in a highly opaque way to a new system that provides for more explicit rationing but leaves it to the government to choose how explicit the new approach to rationing will be. Before the reform of Ukraine's health care financing system, there was a high degree of implicit service rationing, resulting from a wide, open-ended constitutional commitment to free health care and a lack of clear mechanisms to match health care provisions with the budget constraint. The 2017 reform established a rule for defining a minimum benefit package (the PMG) based on transparently defined criteria. However, the law did not prescribe a particular degree of explicitness for the specification of the PMG; this was left to be decided by the PMG regulations to be defined by the CabMin.

The rules governing the PMG design process are quite broad and allow the CabMin considerable discretion in determining the package. The government worked on the initial PMG design in the context of broad and untested procedural regulations. This resulted in substantial changes to the approach during 2019–20 that included growing discretion for the CabMin in decision-making (as compared to the Parliament) and a gradual reduction in decision-making transparency. Examples of the reduction in transparency include the following:

- While the 2017 law stated that the PMG content and pricings would be approved by the Parliament as part of the annual budget law, in 2020 and 2021 this power was delegated to the CabMin. According to the 2017 Law on Financial Guarantees for Health Care Services, the annual PMG budget allocation and the program details—content and tariffs—are supposed to be revised by the NHSU, MoH, and the Ministry of Finance (MoF) and approved by the Parliament as part of the annual budget law. However, the requirement for the Parliament to vote on the PMG content and tariffs was suspended for 2020 and 2021 through amendments to the 2017 law. As a result, the budget laws contain a PMG budget allocation but none of the underlying details; these are approved separately by the CabMin.

- The current rules for technical development of the PMG are broad. The framework law[16] delegates the task of designing the rules for the PMG development to the MoH. These rules, issued by the MoH in July 2019, are broad. The document[17] states that the PMG must include a description of the services with specification of payment mechanisms and tariffs; that it must be designed by the NHSU and approved by the MoH and MoF; and that it must not only reflect national health priorities defined by the MoH but also cover a full menu of essential services selected based on their cost-effectiveness, affordability, and implications for equity and financial protection.

- The MoH does not publicly share the methodology for defining the national health priorities on which the PMG is based. In December 2018, the MoH developed draft national health priorities, including a methodology for their selection with data for each of the criteria, but this draft was never formally released. The formally announced national health priorities were published on the MoH website on January 15, 2020 (Ukraine Ministry of Health News 2020), less than a month before the approval of the PMG. Five priority types of care were listed: treatment of acute myocardial infarction, treatment of acute cerebral stroke, medical assistance to childbirth, neonatal care, and endoscopic cancer screening. These priorities were not formalized in an official document and were not supplied with any details on the methodology used to select them. No further updates of the MoH priorities have been released, so the 2020 list remained effective for the development of the PMG for 2021.

- There is no clear framework to govern the way the NHSU designs the PMG packages and contract specifications. The NHSU develops the draft PMG—including the package structure, service coverage, specification, and pricing—without a clearly defined methodology. The draft PMG was discussed with medical experts and the general public but without a structured framework that would guide such consultations. It is important that this process becomes more transparent and links to carefully designed rules to ensure that it is evidence-based, is free of conflict of interest, and provides relevant stakeholders with sufficient opportunities to give input and make a difference.

- There is no transparent, publicly shared methodology used for PMG costing and price-setting. The tariffs set by the NHSU for the PMG service packages, as well as the program's overall financing need, were defined without a transparent methodology and public access to relevant data. This makes it difficult to assess PMG financing levels and the choices made on service-rationing criteria in the PMG design.

While broader 2018 public financial management (PFM) reforms implied a transition to medium-term budgeting, they were put on hold in 2020, effectively limiting the PMG design process to a one-year horizon, which is too short. The medium-term budgeting framework, introduced in Ukraine in December 2018, enabled the government to initiate strategic PMG financing consultations at a sufficiently early stage. In early 2019, the MoH prepared 2020–22 financing proposals for the full-fledged PMG, broadly identifying the reform pathway. This included an approximate selection of service priority classes to continue supplementing the PMG budget with local revenue by delegating utility cost coverage to the SNGs in the medium term—and the plan to direct the then-expected increase in the PMG allocation into financing priority services and medical goods. However, the 2020–22 whole-of-government budget declaration, which included a three-year horizon for the PMG, was not approved by the CabMin. In 2020, the government entirely suspended the medium-term budgeting rules because of COVID-19–related uncertainties. The suspension was arguably a necessary pandemic response measure, giving the government flexibility in the face of extreme uncertainty. However, this unfortunate coincidence between the crisis and the reform rollout made it harder for the government to commit to the reform trajectory in the forthcoming years.

The government does not approve expenditure ceilings before PMG preparation by the MoH/NHSU. Sector ceilings provided by the MoF to budget spending units to inform the preparation of budget proposals are not approved by the CabMin until it votes on the entire draft budget or the 3-year budget declaration. This means that the ceilings can change significantly throughout the budget preparation process, leaving spending units like the MoH/NHSU without a reliable budget envelope to prepare their proposals. The latest Public Expenditure and Financial Accountability assessment of Ukraine's PFM system notes this as a general budgeting weakness in Ukraine and recommends that the political leadership engage in priority setting at a much earlier stage in the budgeting process (World Bank 2019).

With the overlapping responsibility for health financing, there is no clarity on how the fiduciary risks associated with facility budget deficits are shared between the central and local governments. As Ukraine has transitioned away from supply-side subsidies to providers and toward purchasing services from autonomous providers through the PMG, it has become possible for providers to experience financing gaps, especially if service delivery is inefficient. No law would require either local or central government to cover financing gaps of the autonomous care providers. In particular, local administrations, which own most of the provider facilities, are not required to automatically cover their deficits, and they have a wide scope of alternative options for dealing with loss-making providers. However, SNGs do have the right to subsidize the running costs of their local providers, which softens the budget constraint imposed by the PMG central allocation, undermining incentives for facilities to be more efficient. Inefficient management of the PMG allocation leading to a financial gap is a fiduciary risk, and there is no clarity about which government level is expected to deal with it. For example, while the central government has no direct obligation to address facility-level losses, in 2019 and 2020, the central government provided grants to cover subnational losses arising from the transition to new financing and payment arrangements.

As long as the PMG continues to be developed, budgeted, and costed without clear rationing criteria, rationing of care will continue implicitly, despite the intention of moving toward a more explicit benefit package guaranteed to all Ukrainian residents. The discretion in how explicitly the PMG will be rationed leaves the government with a complex political trade-off. While explicit rationing is more open, transparent, and direct, it is usually more challenging politically as it makes it easier to identify winners and losers. Allocating resources by implicit rationing is an easier approach technically because there is no need to develop rationing criteria and politically because the outcomes are less visible to the public. At the same time, as long as the government continues to fund the PMG without clearly expressed criteria for exclusion and inclusion of individuals and services, rationing within the PMG components will continue implicitly at the level of service providers.

FINDING RESOURCES FOR MAINTAINING AND EXPANDING THE PMG: CONSTRAINTS AND OPPORTUNITIES BEYOND 2021

The overall level of government financing of health care in Ukraine is relatively high for its income level but much lower than in neighboring European Union (EU) countries. The total government spending on health in Ukraine is higher than what would be predicted for its income level. At 3.7 percent of GDP in 2018, the latest available year for Ukraine NHA data, government health spending is higher than the LMIC average of 2.78 percent and close to upper-middle-income countries (UMICs) at 4.0 percent and non-OECD high-income countries (HICs) at 3.86 percent. At the same time, this level of public health funding is lower than Ukraine's EU neighbors, most of which are OECD HICs (6.51 percent in 2017). For example, public health spending is 4.5 percent of GDP in Poland, 4.8 percent of GDP in Estonia, and 5.3 percent of GDP in the Slovak Republic.

Expanding the PMG will require additional funding, but not all of the available resource generation options would be equally effective and some may entail risks. It is vital that the annual budget allocations to the PMG are sufficient to cover the provision of services included by law in the PMG benefit package, or there will inevitably be service rationing, undermining the guarantee to care provided by the government of Ukraine to the Ukrainian people. Several options may be considered individually or in combination to secure additional resources for the PMG. First, there is the possibility of expanding the overall fiscal envelope either through new taxes or new debt. Second, it may be possible to reallocate resources from other functions or programs by deprioritizing other sectors. The third option is to deprioritize other (non-PMG) health spending within the health sector. Fourth, it might be possible to reconsider the intergovernmental revenue-sharing arrangement. However, if the government decides to shift the responsibility for PMG utility financing from SNGs to the central level and revises the intergovernmental revenue arrangement to reflect the change, this will not expand the financing envelope but merely shift financing responsibilities across government tiers. Fifth, it would be possible to expand the PMG by efficiency gains, including better PFM. Finally, if the government considers introducing a cost-sharing arrangement—co-payments for services covered by the PMG and supplementary payments for noncovered services—this may entail considerable risks of worsening Ukraine's heavy reliance on OOPs; it may involve high administrative costs and may weaken strategic purchasing if not strictly regulated. Each of these options is discussed in turn below.

The government has committed to spending significantly more on health, and the PMG particularly, in 2020–21, but it remains to be seen whether this trend will be sustained in the longer term. Despite the economic recession associated with the COVID-19 pandemic, the government significantly increased consolidated budget spending on health in the 2020 budget, bringing it up to 4.24 percent of GDP. This does not include health expenditures accounted outside the health function in the Classification of the Functions of Government, which would make the NHA total even bigger—the highest level in Ukraine's recent times. Stronger prioritization of health was expected to continue in 2021. Although there were no data on subnational budget plans for 2021 when this report was being prepared, the central budget health allocation, including health transfers to the SNGs, was approved at a level that is 14.2 percent (Ukrainian hryvnia [UAH] 20 billion) higher than the 2020 plan and corresponds to 3.6–3.8 percent of GDP, depending on GDP growth scenario. In the approved 2021 budget, the PMG was funded at a level that represents a 20.3 percent increase compared to 2020 for the services accounted for in the PMG—services purchased by the NHSU, the health grant used by the SNGs to pay for specialized and emergency care in the first quarter of 2020, and the transitional grant to support loss-making facilities. These increases were expected to be funded from new borrowing in 2020–21 and an increase in the health spending share in the central budget in 2021. In addition, in 2020, the NHSU started to use the PMG contract specifications and tariffs to increase efficiency gains in the provision of services within the program—a new policy facing a range of technical and political challenges that are discussed in the next sections.

Expansion of the fiscal envelope (new debt and new taxes)

Even before the COVID-19 pandemic, Ukraine's economic growth rate was insufficient to sustain its debt without a tight fiscal policy in the medium term. Between 2012 and 2015, Ukraine experienced an economic recession, culminating in a deep macro-fiscal crisis with GDP falling by –17.2 percent year-on-year in 2015 (see figure 2.6).

Before 2015, the government maintained large deficits to boost pensions and salaries—including in health care—rapidly building up public debt (see figure 2.7).

As the crisis hit in 2014–15, this debt grew to 99.9 percent of GDP, resulting in a sharp depreciation of currency and bank recapitalization needs. The government restored stability by removing major structural imbalances, such as quasi-fiscal deficits in the energy sector, and shifting to a flexible exchange rate regime to reduce the current account deficit. It also sharply reduced the general government deficit from 4.9 percent of GDP in 2014 to 1.8 percent in 2017, as presented in figure 2.8.

FIGURE 2.6

Real GDP change, year-on-year

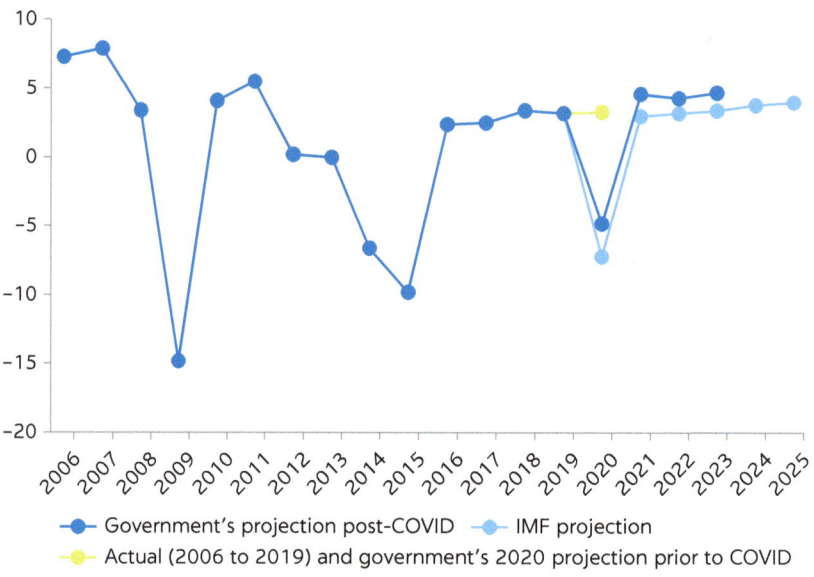

Sources: State Treasury Service of Ukraine; IMF 2020.

FIGURE 2.7

Public debt, including guarantees, as a percentage of GDP

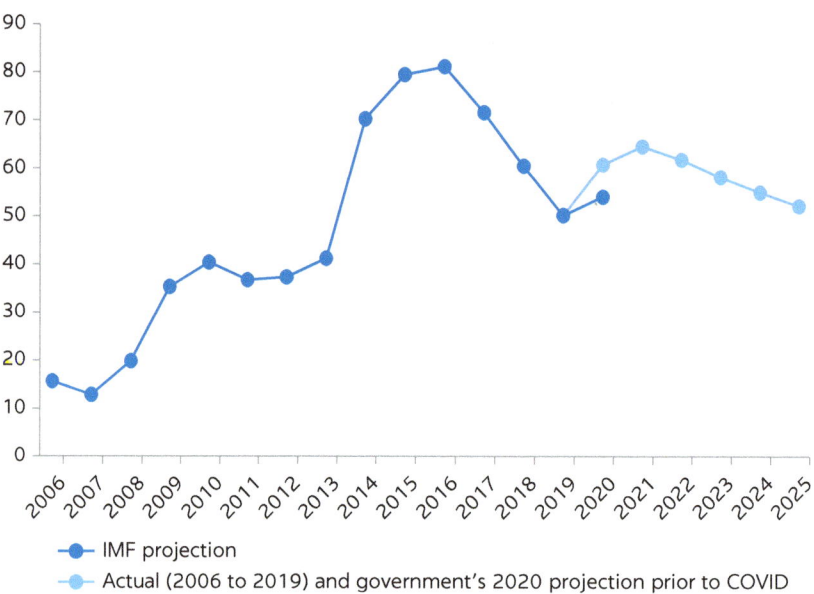

Sources: State Treasury Service of Ukraine; IMF 2020.

Throughout 2015–19, consolidated expenditures grew more moderately than revenues, leaving space for debt repayment, and consolidated spending started to contract in 2018 (figure 2.9). By 2019, the stock of debt was reduced by almost half to only 56.1 percent of GDP, but economic growth remained insufficient to sustain this remaining debt without further fiscal consolidation. In 2019, the International Monetary Fund (IMF) advised Ukraine to maintain a primary surplus of 1.0–1.5 percent of GDP, unless the economy could be boosted through a better business climate and anticorruption reforms.

FIGURE 2.8

Budget balance of the general government, including funds, as a percentage of GDP

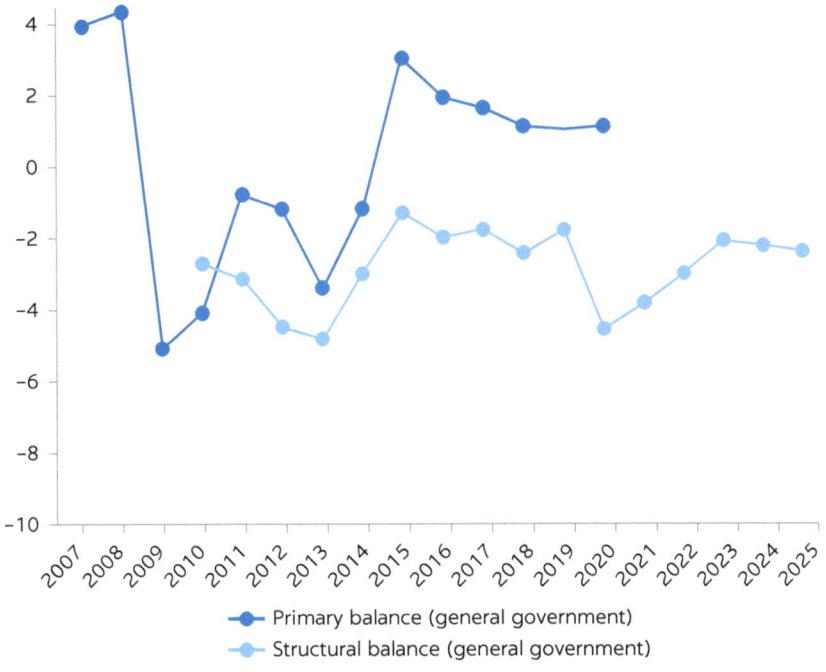

Sources: State Treasury Service of Ukraine; IMF 2020.

FIGURE 2.9

Revenue and expenditures of the consolidated budget as a percentage of GDP

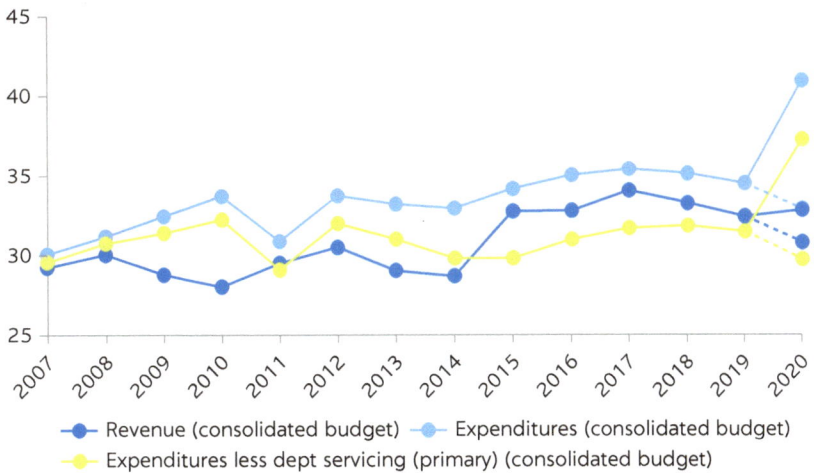

Sources: State Treasury Service of Ukraine; IMF 2020.

In 2019–20, Ukraine's GDP started to contract, which was further exacerbated by the COVID-19 pandemic. After slowing down since mid-2019, the economy started contracting, and in January 2020, it was down by 0.5 percent compared to January 2019. Reacting to the COVID-19 pandemic, the recession intensified. The government's latest official projection of the 2020 annual contraction, issued on April 23, 2020, was −4.8 percent, while the IMF's more recent forecast (IMF 2020) is −7.2 percent, illustrated earlier in figure 2.6, showing the steepest decline among all European emerging and developing economies,[18] except Croatia.

Responding to the new economic crisis, the government expected to run a short-term deficit of at least 4.5 percent of GDP in 2020, letting the public debt return to the 2017–18 level. The government's budget amendments, introduced in April 2020 in response to the pandemic, assumed that the consolidated deficit would grow from 2.3 percent of GDP originally planned for this year to 8.4 percent of GDP in 2020, with the primary balance turning from a surplus of 0.9 percent of GDP into a 4.7 percent GDP deficit (see figure 2.10). The IMF projections as of October 2020 assumed that actual spending in 2020 would be much lower than these estimates, with the general government deficit increasing to only 4.5 percent of GDP, as presented earlier in figure 2.8.[19] But even with this lower estimated deficit, Ukraine's public debt was still expected to grow to 65.7 percent of GDP in 2020, close to the 2017–18 average of 66.3 percent.

In the medium term, the IMF forecasted that even if growth resumed in 2021, bringing debt back under control would require the government to consolidate spending immediately and bring it down to the 2015 levels by 2025. The IMF expected that from 2021, Ukraine's economy would start to recover, returning to its 2018 growth rate (3.4 percent) by 2023. However, this forecast assumed that the government would start to consolidate spending in 2021, gradually reducing general government expenditures (including funds) from 46.9 percent of GDP in 2020 to 43.0 percent in 2025—returning to the 2015 level, shown in figure 2.11. This would allow trimming the deficits and bringing the overall debt stock to the pre-COVID level by 2025, as illustrated earlier in figure 2.7.

The central budget approved for 2021 assumed that total spending would contract compared to the 2020 plan despite continued deficits. The 2021 Budget Law approved a central budget deficit of 5.5 percent of GDP and a primary deficit of 2.0 percent (no estimates for consolidated or general deficit

FIGURE 2.10

Consolidated budget balance: All tiers as a percentage of GDP

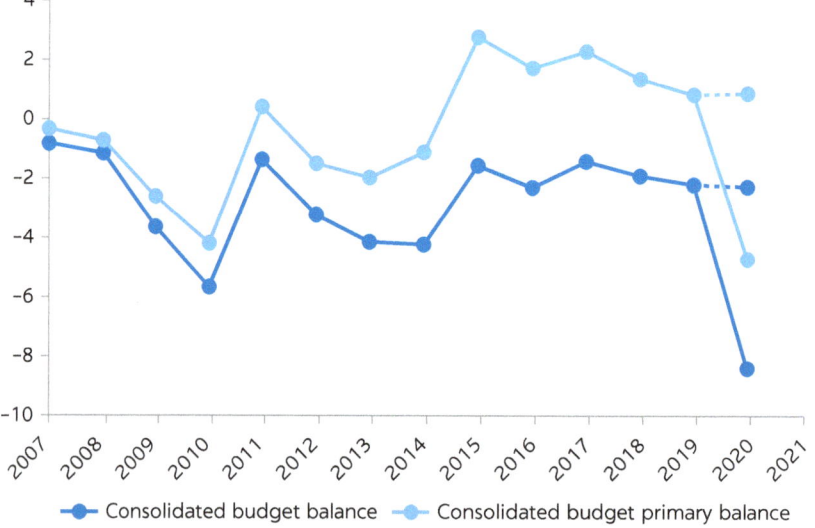

Sources: State Treasury Service of Ukraine; IMF 2020.

FIGURE 2.11

Revenue and expenditures of the general government, including funds, as a percentage of GDP

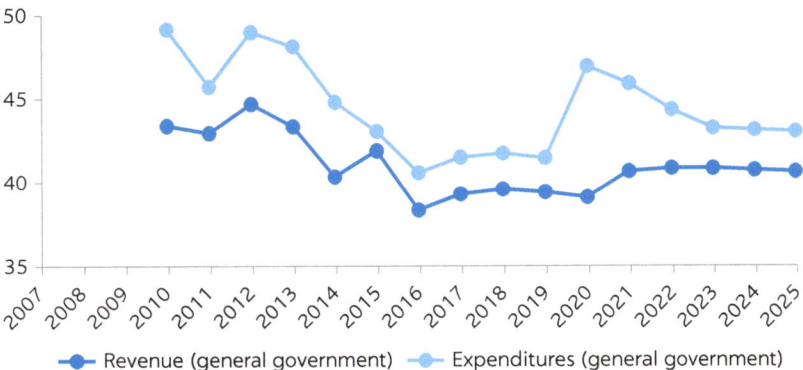

Sources: State Treasury Service of Ukraine; IMF 2020.

were available at the time of writing this report). While this represented a decrease compared to the 2020 plan (7.6 percent and 4.1 percent, respectively), the central budget was still expected to remain in primary deficit, continuing the post-COVID fiscal expansion. At the same time, central-level spending would decrease from 32.5 percent of GDP in the 2020 Plan to 29.5 percent of GDP, as laid out in table 2.1. In other words, the central government expected to spend less in 2021 compared to the 2020 plan, even though its budget would be in deficit, leading to higher debt. At the same time, compared to 2019, spending would be significantly higher—as would be the deficit; in 2019, the central budget had a primary surplus of 1 percent of GDP.

Despite the overall contraction of central expenditures compared to the 2020 plan (as a percentage of GDP), central health spending (including transfers) was expected to significantly increase to 3.6–3.8 percent of GDP. Within the central government expenditures approved for 2021, spending on health, including grants to the SNGs earmarked for health spending, was expected to grow by UAH 20 billion—from UAH 141 billion to UAH 161 billion—compared to the 2020 plan as presented in table 2.2. This would represent an increase from 3.5 percent of GDP to 3.6 percent of GDP, based on the latest available government GDP projection; if growth in 2021 is slower, as was projected by the IMF, planned central health spending would amount to 3.8 percent of GDP. As will be discussed in the next section, this increase should become possible by expanding the share of health in the central budget, while reducing the relative priority of other major functions listed in table 2.1: social protection, social security and judiciary, and defense.

Under current growth projections, central health allocations may grow by 33–41 percent by 2025, but this requires the government to maintain central health spending at 3.6–3.8 percent of GDP. Simulating possible developments in the longer term, if the central government keeps the share of health spending at 3.6 percent of GDP (Scenario 2 in table 2.2), under the IMF GDP growth projections, nominal allocation to health would grow to UAH 215.6 billion, or by 33 percent by 2025. By spending 3.8 percent of GDP (Scenario 3), it may reach UAH 226.6 billion by that year—growing by 41 percent. But if Ukraine's GDP grows faster than predicted by the IMF and in line with the government's current forecast, central budget health spending may reach UAH 207.3 billion under

TABLE 2.1 Central government spending, including transfers

	EXPENDITURES[a] AS A PERCENTAGE OF GDP								EXPENDITURES[a] AS A PERCENTAGE OF THE TOTAL CENTRAL BUDGET WITH TRANSFERS							
	2015	2016	2017	2018	2019	2020[b]	2020[c]	2021[d]	2015	2016	2017	2018	2019	2020[b]	2020[c]	2021[d]
Public administration	5.2	5.0	4.8	4.6	4.3	4.3	5.0	4.8	18.1	17.4	17.2	16.7	15.9	16.4	15.4	16.3
including debt servicing	4.2	4.0	3.7	3.2	3.0	3.1	3.6	3.5	14.6	14.0	13.2	11.7	11.1	11.9	11.2	11.9
Defense	2.6	2.5	2.5	2.7	2.7	2.6	3.0	2.6	9.0	8.7	8.9	9.8	9.9	10.0	9.3	9.0
Security and judiciary	2.7	3.0	2.9	3.3	3.6	3.3	3.9	3.7	9.5	10.5	10.5	11.9	13.2	12.6	12.1	12.5
Economic activities	1.9	1.5	1.8	2.3	2.3	2.7	4.2	2.9	6.6	5.1	6.3	8.2	8.4	10.3	13.0	9.9
Environment	0.2	0.2	0.2	0.2	0.2	0.2	0.2	0.2	0.7	0.7	0.6	0.5	0.6	0.7	0.6	0.7
Housing and utilities	0.0	0.0	0.1	0.0	0.0	0.0	0.0	0.0	0.0	0.0	0.2	0.0	0.0	0.0	0.0	0.0
Health care	3.2	2.4	2.6	2.5	2.5	2.5	3.5	3.6	11.0	8.4	9.4	8.9	9.1	9.6	10.9	12.1
Culture and sports	0.3	0.2	0.3	0.3	0.3	0.3	0.3	0.4	1.2	0.7	0.9	1.0	1.0	1.2	0.8	1.5
Education	3.7	3.3	3.1	3.0	3.1	3.2	3.6	3.7	12.9	11.6	11.1	10.8	11.6	12.3	10.9	12.6
Social protection	8.7	10.3	9.1	8.2	7.5	6.6	8.2	7.0	29.8	36.0	32.4	29.6	27.8	25.1	25.2	23.7
Block grants	0.4	0.3	0.7	0.7	0.6	0.5	0.5	0.5	1.3	1.0	2.6	2.6	2.4	1.8	1.7	1.7
Total	29.0	28.7	28.1	27.7	27.0	26.2	32.5	29.5	100.0	100.0	100.0	100.0	100.0	100.0	100.0	100.0

Sources: State Treasury Service of Ukraine (actuals); Annual Budget Laws (plan); CabMin (GDP); IMF 2020 (IMF projections).
Note: GDP = gross domestic product; IMF = International Monetary Fund; SNG = subnational government.
a. Totals for each function include grants to SNGs related to this function.
b. Initial plan.
c. Post–COVID-19 plan.
d. Budget revised as of November 2021.

TABLE 2.2 Central government health spending, including transfers, projections to 2025

YEAR	GDP, CURRENT PRICES (UAH BILLIONS)[a]		AS % OF GDP ACTUAL/PLAN[b]		SIMULATIONS			CURRENT PRICES (UAH, BILLIONS) ACTUAL/PLAN	IMF GDP PROJECTIONS SIMULATIONS			GOV GDP PROJECTIONS		
	IMF	GOV	IMF	GOV	1	2	3	GOV	1	2	3	1	2	3
2015	1,988.5	1,988.5	3.2	3.2	—	—	—	63.3	—	—	—	—	—	—
2016	2,385.4	2,385.4	2.4	2.4	—	—	—	57.2	—	—	—	—	—	—
2017	2,982.9	2,983.9	2.6	2.6	—	—	—	78.7	—	—	—	—	—	—
2018	3,560.6	3,558.7	2.5	2.5	—	—	—	87.4	—	—	—	—	—	—
2019	3,974.6	3,978.4	2.5	2.5	—	—	—	97.7	—	—	—	—	—	—
2020	3,869.7	3,985.5	3.6	3.5	—	—	—	141.0	—	—	—	—	—	—
2021	4,205.1	4,505.9	3.8	3.6	—	—	—	161.0	—	—	—	—	—	—
2022	4,571.4	5,089.4	—	—	3.5	3.6	3.8	—	158.9	166.5	175.1	176.9	185.4	194.9
2023	4,972.7	5,689.7	—	—	3.4	3.6	3.8	—	168.0	181.2	190.4	192.3	207.3	217.9
2024	5,420.5	—	—	—	3.3	3.6	3.8	—	177.9	197.5	207.6	—	—	—
2025	5,918.3	—	—	—	3.2	3.6	3.8	—	188.5	215.6	226.6	—	—	—

Sources: State Treasury Service of Ukraine (actuals); Annual Budget Laws (plan); CabMin (GDP); IMF 2020 (IMF projections).

Note: — = data not available; GDP = gross domestic product; GOV = government; IMF = International Monetary Fund; SNG = subnational government.

a. GDP projections being 2020.

b. Budget totals reflect actual execution statistics for 2015–19, planned amounts for 2020–21, and projections beyond 2022.

Scenario 2 and UAH 217.9 billion under Scenario 3 by 2023. However, if general expenditure consolidation to the 2015 level, as suggested by the IMF, is translated into an equal, gradual reduction of spending on health (Scenario 1), the nominal health allocation might actually contract in 2022 or grow modestly.

Regardless of the economic trajectory in the next few years, extra revenue could be collected through improved tax and customs administration. Ukraine already redistributes a significant share of its GDP through state taxation and spending. In 2019, even after the significant postcrisis fiscal consolidation, the share of public spending in Ukraine was 41.51 percent, which is higher than the average for advanced economies. This makes it difficult to extract additional taxes without a significant accompanying improvement in the quality of public services in the larger role of the state. On the other hand, the 2019 assessment by the IMF suggested that revenue collection could be significantly expanded through reforms in the organization, management, and oversight of the tax and customs systems.

It is also possible to consider additional health-related taxation, including higher taxes on alcohol consumption and tobacco consumption, as well as introducing taxes on saturated fat, salt, and sugar consumption:

- Alcohol taxation. Higher alcohol taxation is currently not on the table, but it might be considered in the longer term, both from fiscal and health perspectives. On the one hand, alcohol consumption in Ukraine declined substantially between 2010 and 2016, from 14.3 liters of pure alcohol per year to 8.6 liters, or by 40 percent, at which point drinking became less prevalent in Ukraine than in the EU13 countries, the United Kingdom, Spain, Moldova, Belarus, or Russia.[20] On the other hand, alcohol remains one of the leading mortality risk factors for young adults 15 to 49 years old, causing 31.8 percent of deaths in this age group, with 35.1 percent of deaths among men.

- Tobacco taxation. In the past decade, Ukraine has been highly successful in using tobacco taxation to create new budget revenue and improve public health outcomes. The government has raised tobacco taxes regularly since 2008, most actively during 2014–16 to around 40 percent annually. In 2017, it approved a 7-year plan to continue raising tobacco taxes by approximately 20 percent every year until 2024 to ultimately harmonize the tobacco tax structure and increase rates to the EU minimum to counteract fraud and illegal cross-border trade. As a result, revenues from tobacco taxes grew from 1.18 percent of GDP in 2011 to 1.55 percent of GDP in 2020. These significant tax increases, combined with a range of antismoking measures, have decreased the prevalence of tobacco use from 28.4 percent in 2010 to 23.0 percent in 2017, from 49.9 percent to 40.1 percent among men. However, as of 2019, the MoF expected that the tobacco tax proceeds would continue to expand in the medium term despite reduced consumption, which makes it a win-win strategy, bringing budget revenue along with public health benefits.

- Saturated fat, salt, and sugar taxation. While mortality attribution to tobacco and alcohol consumption is declining, obesity is a growing risk in Ukraine. The share of mortality attributed to the high body mass index steadily increased in the past decades, from 12.6 percent of all deaths in 1990 to 15.5 percent in 2014. Another factor is the growing share of mortality caused by diets high in sugar-sweetened beverages, processed meat, red meat, and trans-fatty acids. Even though each of these risks is responsible for less than 1 percent of all deaths, their attribution has been steadily increasing since 2001. The WHO 2018 analysis of noncommunicable disease (NCDs) country profiles confirms this trend since the early 2000s: a substantial decline in tobacco smoking, steady improvement in the blood pressure levels, but a continuous rise in obesity prevalence. Taxing consumption of saturated fat, salt, and sugar is one of the promising tools to address this health concern and also create more budgetary space for health care financing.

Increasing the budgetary share of health spending

From 2014 and up to the pre-COVID 2020 budget, Ukraine increasingly deprioritized health spending within the consolidated government budget. Throughout the years of expansionary fiscal policy in 2007–13, the government kept the health share of consolidated health spending at around 12 percent, but because of the growing envelope, the level of health spending increased to 4.04 percent of GDP by 2013 (see figure 2.12). In 2014–15, the share of health spending started to shrink, giving space to crisis-related priorities—social protection, defense, and debt servicing—falling to 9 percent in 2016. Combined with the decreasing level of state spending, health expenditures decreased to just 3.2 percent of GDP in 2016. But even once the 2014–15 crisis subsided and the pressures for emergency social safety measures and debt servicing started to decline, the share of health had not recovered and remained at 9.2 percent in the pre-COVID 2020 budget. Moreover, health spending kept falling as a share of GDP to 3 percent in the pre-COVID 2020 budget, because the government started consolidating the overall envelope again to deal with the revenue decline developing since 2017.

FIGURE 2.12

Health care funding levels, 2007–20

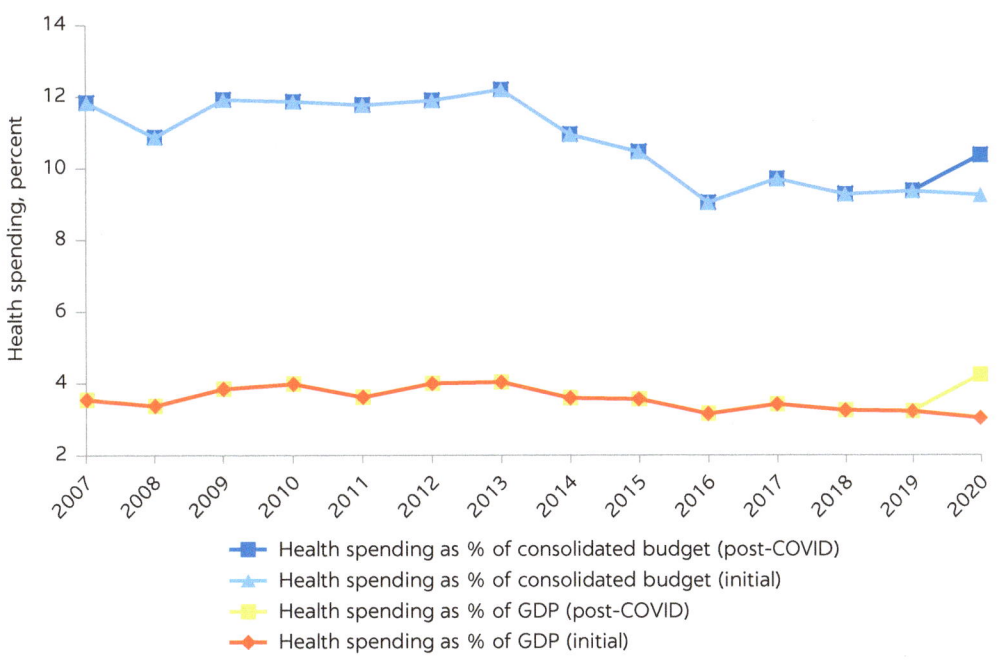

Sources: State Treasury Service of Ukraine (actuals); Annual Budget Laws (plan); CabMin (GDP)

Figure 2.13 shows that despite the deteriorating fiscal situation, the share of spending on education, economic activities, defense, and security and the judiciary significantly expanded.

The 2020 COVID-19 budget amendments sharply increased the share of the consolidated government budget going to health to 10.4 percent, equivalent to 4.24 percent of GDP. Reacting to COVID-19, the central government increased the planned allocation to health care, including earmarked health grants, by 1.0 percent of GDP, which helped expand the share of health within the central budget from 9.6 percent to 10.9 percent. The SNGs also increased their health care allocations funded from their revenue on top of earmarked health grants by 0.2 percent of GDP. Together, these measures helped raise planned consolidated health spending to the highest level in recent times (figure 2.12). However, investment in some nonhealth infrastructures received an even higher priority—for example, as shown in figure 2.13, consolidated spending on economic activities grew by 1.6 percent of GDP (within which, spending on roads increased by 2.1 percent of GDP).

The 2021 budget further increases central spending on health to 12.1 percent of total government spending, equivalent to 3.6 percent of GDP. At the time of writing, though the 2021 Budget Law containing the central budget health allocation was already approved, the SNGs had not yet approved their budgets, making it impossible to establish the consolidated 2021 health budget projections. At the central level, the 2021 budget signals a slight change in functional priorities. As already stated, central spending on health, including transfers to SNGs, would

FIGURE 2.13

Largest functions as a percentage of consolidated expenditures, 2007–20

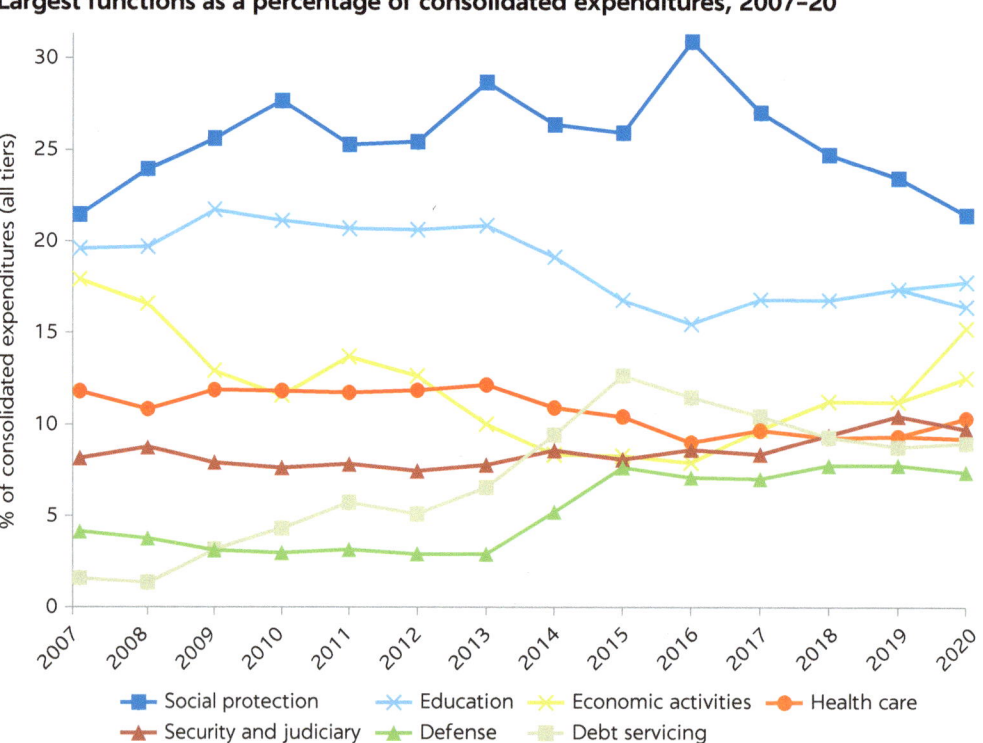

Sources: State Treasury Service of Ukraine; State Statistics Service of Ukraine.

continue to grow strongly as a share of spending, from 10.9 percent to 12.1 percent—and as a share of GDP, from 3.5 percent to 3.6 percent. The only other function experiencing a similar increase is education.

Comparisons with the OECD countries suggest that there might still be room to grow the share of the government's budget going to health. In a broad comparison to OECD countries, most of whose health care systems are based on a strong role of the government in health care financing and also cover long-term care, the share of health spending in Ukraine is predictably lower, by 2.5 times, 11.5 percentage points in 2019. On the other hand, Ukraine allocates a significantly higher budgetary share to internal security (+3.9 percentage points), social protection (+3.8 percentage points), and education (+2.0 percentage points) compared to the OECD average.

Looking ahead, reconsideration of the importance of health versus functional priorities should involve a whole-of-government spending review using a scenario-based, medium-term macro-fiscal outlook. Significant reprioritization of government spending requires the review to detect inefficiencies and evaluate possibilities for resource reallocation across sectors. A spending review to assess the Ukrainian context for potential functional reprioritization would also depend significantly on the future economic outlook, the fiscal policies the government will choose in reaction to the crisis, and the approach to fiscal consolidation once the crisis subsides.

Increasing the budgetary share of PMG within the health budget

Because other health programs could not reasonably be cut back without dire consequences for population health, the scope for the expansion of the share of PMG in the health budget beyond that which is already planned is marginal. As discussed above, the PMG purchased through the NHSU is currently absorbing about 53 percent of the consolidated health budget. Another 21 percent of the consolidated health budget is spent on PMG-related utility and capital costs through the SNGs (and therefore reflected separately in the budget) and on some additional services that should be migrated to the PMG as part of the original reform design. This will substantially increase the budgetary share of the PMG within the health budget. The scope for significantly expanding PMG funding within the current health budget is therefore relatively small. However, a range of health programs could still be revisited through specific spending reviews. For instance, in 2019, the MoH conducted two spending reviews on some of its central programs, but the reports were not approved or taken forward by the ministry.

Rebalancing the intergovernmental revenue-sharing arrangement

Sharing the PMG funding responsibilities across government tiers may be fine-tuned in the long run to increase efficiency, but it would not increase the PMG resource envelope:

- Local discretionary supplementation of the PMG running costs is already near the level before the reform, approximately 8 percent of the total amount of spending on PMG services. As discussed earlier in this report, the reform left the SNGs with the right to supplement PMG running costs. Before the reform, when the SNGs were paying for the bulk of health services funded through central health grants, they had traditionally supplemented central grants with a substantial portion of local revenue, nearly 25 percent of the total health budget, as shown in table 2.3. Within this local supplement, about one-third covered utility costs, and another one-third was invested in capital costs. After the reform, subnational financing of utility costs and capital expenditures became mandatory, but the SNGs were given discretion as to whether they wanted to continue to pay the rest of their traditional budget supplement. In essence, their expenditure responsibility was reduced by about UAH 10 billion as of 2020. While there was no matching reconsideration of the tax assignment responsibility between government tiers, the MoF reduced the size of one of the three core block grants available as delegated revenue for local budgets in 2020 by UAH 4 billion. In that year, the size of the local supplementary financing decreased by UAH 6.1 billion between 2019 and the pre-COVID-19 2020 plan. In other words, having been given the discretion to do so, and having a reduced delegated revenue base, the SNGs continued to voluntarily supplement around UAH 4 billion of the PMG running costs. Moreover, facing COVID-19 costs, the SNGs have significantly increased their contribution to health expenditures, which grew to nearly the level prior to the reform.

• Local supplementation of the PMG running costs can lead to inefficiencies, but these can be addressed through a set of specific national policy tools. On the one hand, the practice of local supplementation of the PMG budget may lead to inefficiencies. Local politics in both centralized and decentralized systems tend to lead to advocacy to retain inefficient, low-occupancy, and low-quality facilities in small hospitals, usually in rural and small-town locations. It also

TABLE 2.3 Intergovernmental financing of health care, 2015–20

HEALTH SPENDING	2015	2016	2017	2018	2019	2020 PLAN PRE-COVID	2020 PLAN POST-COVID
Consolidated budget (UAH billions)	**71.0**	**75.5**	**102.4**	**115.9**	**128.4**	**138.5**	**169.0**
Central spending (state budget health expenditures, including health grants)	63.3	57.2	78.7	87.4	97.7	113.9	141.0
Local co-pay (local budget health spending, excluding health grants)	7.7	18.3	23.7	28.4	30.7	24.6	28.0
Consolidated budget (percent of GDP)	**3.57**	**3.17**	**3.43**	**3.26**	**3.23**	**3.04**	**4.24**
Central spending (state budget health expenditures, including health grants)	3.19	2.40	2.64	2.46	2.46	2.50	3.54
Local co-pay (local budget health spending, excluding health grants)	0.39	0.77	0.79	0.80	0.77	0.54	0.70
Consolidated budget (percent of total consolidated expenditures)	**100.00**	**100.00**	**100.00**	**100.00**	**100.00**	**100.00**	**100.00**
Central spending (state budget health expenditures, including health grants)	89.21	75.80	76.86	75.47	76.09	82.24	83.43
Local co-pay (local budget health spending, excluding health grants)	10.79	24.20	23.14	24.53	23.91	17.76	16.57

Source: State Treasury Service of Ukraine.

encourages inefficient competition to invest in high-tech and tertiary facilities among city hospitals in larger population centers. There is often an incentive for local politicians to advocate to retain excessive numbers of employees in their facilities—particularly in nonclinical, lower-skilled roles. On the other hand, it is important that the SNGs as hospital owners face some financial risk; this will stimulate efficiency improvements. To counteract local political incentives for maintaining inefficiency, Ukraine would benefit from introducing some specific policy instruments to address this problem. This could include, for example, conditional grants from the central government to SNGs, including potentially ones linked to progress in improving hospital performance. Ukraine could also consider introducing limits on the level or duration of SNG subsidies for operating costs of facilities. In addition, SNGs may be less likely to retain loss-making hospitals if health facility master plans, developed jointly by national and local governments, were to become binding on public sector investment.

- It may be possible to reconsider intragovernmental revenue assignment if the central government takes over responsibility for the PMG utility costs—increasing efficiency but not leading to an increase in resources available to the PMG. It has been stated in this report that the ongoing delegation to the SNGs of the responsibility for covering utility costs creates a range of inefficiencies. This arrangement discriminates against private providers that compete for NHSU contracts without utility costs being subsidized by the public purse. It also complicates costing for estimating realistic case rates, as will be discussed in chapter 3. The current arrangement was designed as a temporary solution in December 2016 to address mounting crisis-related spending pressures at the central level—for example, covering social protection, defense, and debt servicing—in the context of a decentralization reform, which delegated a significant amount of revenue to subnational administrations. It remains possible, albeit technically and politically challenging, to reconsider this approach, concentrating full responsibility for the PMG utility costs within the central budget with a matching reduction in the amount of revenue shared with the local budgets.

Efficiency gains

Improved spending efficiency is an important source of extra resources for the health sector in both developing and advanced economies. For poorer countries with a low level of government health spending, enhanced efficiency is an obvious opportunity to achieve better outcomes. But even among OECD countries, the fast-growing level of public investment in health in the past decade was one reason to critically assess the value for money in the health budget and seek ways to achieve more with less through better system management. Even now, richer countries remain highly diverse in their health spending efficiency levels.

Ukraine's health care system relies on an excessive and inefficient network of health care facilities and excessively relies on expensive hospital care. Despite visible reorganization during 2008–19, especially for tuberculosis (TB) care, hospitals are still abundant and inefficient. The total bed density in Ukraine declined significantly in the past decade, bringing it closer to the EU13 average, but bed density is still excessive, as is the number of hospitals.[21] Even for acute hospitals, excluding TB and psychiatric care, there are more hospitals per 1 million population in Ukraine than in the neighboring countries, including the EU13.[22] However, Ukraine's hospitals are relatively large, and their occupancy is comparatively high, especially in the cities. This reflects the high rate of hospitalizations in Ukraine and the high average length of hospital stay. The hospital discharge rate fell by 16.2 percent in the past decade, bringing Ukraine close to the Slovak Republic and Poland. The decline in hospitalization rates was especially visible in non-acute TB and psychiatric care. The average length of stay (ALOS) is also decreasing, but the reduction is marginal for psychiatric care, obstetric care, and especially TB. Despite the recent decline, ALOS in Ukraine is still much higher than in the European comparator countries such as Poland, Estonia, the Slovak Republic, and Romania.

Hospitals in Ukraine are poorly equipped, and the level of utilization of key medical procedures is low. The number of computerized tomography (CT) scanners and magnetic resonance imaging (MRI) units per 1 million population is remarkably lower than in EU13 countries.[23] The utilization of surgical procedures in Ukraine is substantially lower than in comparator countries, and the number of inpatient surgical procedures per one surgical group specialist in Ukraine is also substantially lower than in other countries of Europe. Operations that are most common in Europe—cataract surgery and coronary angioplasty—are performed much less frequently in Ukraine.

The weak role of the PHC and lack of effective integration between care levels prevent earlier and cheaper treatment of NCDs. One of the reasons behind the overreliance on hospital care in Ukraine is the weakness of the PHC sector, which has been historically underfunded and underutilized. The lack of integration between lower and higher levels of care to facilitate upward and downward patient referral and the weak role of the PHC also play a part. This contributes to the late detection of NCDs and prevents patients from receiving treatment and staying in care at a sufficiently early stage when providing relevant services is cheaper and more effective.

The introduction of the PMG opens an opportunity for significant efficiency improvement through greater spending flexibility, output-based contracts, and provider autonomy. The overarching lesson from other countries is that extracting more value from a given expenditure envelope requires budgeting rules that ensure sufficient flexibility, policy orientation, and accountability. In Ukraine, prior to the 2017 health reform, even though the budget was approved by programs formally linked to results, spending units were constrained by rigid input-based spending norms. The introduction of the PMG is opening an opportunity to finally apply program-based budgeting in a meaningful way. Within this newly created massive program, the NHSU has received an unprecedented degree of discretion in the appropriation of funds, including the flexibility to reallocate resources across major service types and purchase services based on performance-oriented contracts. Importantly, the shift to contracting services from autonomous providers (public not-for-profit enterprises and private facilities) released spending units from centrally mandated, inputs-based norms, such as staff salary schedules.

Another tool for the NHSU to stimulate hospital rightsizing and productivity is to gradually transition toward case-based payments for inpatient care. The 2017 reform has opened an opportunity for the NHSU to use a wide range of new payment methods for PMG services to increase spending efficiency. In particular, the 2017 Law on Financial Guarantees for Health Care Services introduced the possibility of case-rate reimbursement for services, which is a highly promising tool to stimulate hospital rightsizing and more efficient use of resources within the facilities. Paying for inpatient health care services based on the case mix, in particular through a system of diagnosis-related groups, allows the purchaser to link reimbursement to the hospital workload. It also incentivizes hospitals to contain costs per case by fixing the amount paid for each clinically and economically similar case. Given the excessive size and low productivity of Ukraine's hospital network, incorporating case-rate payment elements into an NHSU purchasing model is an opportunity to expand the budgetary space for the PMG via efficiency gains.

Cost-sharing

Introducing patient cost-sharing undermines access and financial protection and can erode the strategic purchasing function; if introduced, cost-sharing will need to be accompanied by measures to protect against these risks. The government is considering introducing cost-sharing—co-payments for services covered by the PMG and supplementary payments for noncovered services—to permit an expanded range of services and choice of amenities for those who can afford to pay more. Cost-sharing entails considerable risk of adverse consequences: it could worsen Ukraine's already heavy reliance on OOPs through formal and informal payments, involve significant administrative costs, and weaken strategic purchasing if not strictly regulated. It is not realistic to expect that the introduction of cost-sharing will permit an expanded range of services to be covered by the PMG without undermining the PMG's objective of ensuring equitable access to services. If cost-sharing is introduced, it should be in the form of small, flat co-payments that are subject to annual caps and limited to selected services (certainly excluding preventive care to promote its utilization). Poor households should be exempt from all co-payments, and percentage co-payments should be avoided. The design of any co-payment policy should be as simple as possible to ensure that people can easily navigate the health system and do not face administrative barriers to benefiting from protective measures. In addition to co-payments for covered services, the government is considering allowing supplementary payments as a means of encouraging private providers to supply PMG services. If implemented, supplementary payments should be limited to aspects of service delivery that are not directly associated with the clinical quality of care, like a single room in hospital (extra billing). Health care providers should not be allowed to ask patients to pay in addition to co-payments for covered services (balance billing). The implementation of co-payments for covered services and supplementary payments for noncovered services requires careful regulation and active monitoring to avoid creating inequities (including potential discrimination against people who are exempt from co-payments or do not make supplementary payments), reducing financial protection, and undermining strategic purchasing incentives.

RECOMMENDATIONS

Short term

- Clarify the political process for the design and expansion of the PMG benefit package (including its approval) to make it more transparent, explicit, and participatory.

- Implement a process and associated rules within the health sector to ensure a medium-term perspective in the definition of the PMG benefit package and its budgeting, even if the government-wide medium-term investment framework remains suspended.
- Introduce rules for the CabMin to provide reliable budget ceilings in advance of the annual budget preparation process, not only for each sector, such as health, but ideally also for priority programs such as the PMG within each sectoral budget; this would need to be a government-wide measure.
- Introduce policy instruments to address the risks of continued inefficiencies resulting from the SNGs using local revenue to retain inefficient, low-occupancy, and low-quality facilities in small hospitals in rural and small-town locations, and inefficient competition to invest in high-tech and tertiary facilities among city hospitals in larger population centers. These instruments could include regulatory powers for the center to help direct SNG investments in a way that is more efficient from a system-wide perspective. Additionally, the center can use financing instruments such as grants to incentivize more appropriate investments at the local level.
- Consider shifting financing responsibilities for utilities from the SNGs to the central budget, paid by the NHSU through the PMG budget directly to facilities. This would reduce inefficiencies, strengthen the principle of "money-follows-the patient," and help level the playing field for private providers.
- Continue and extend the MoH's practice of undertaking detailed, health sector–specific spending reviews, together with the MoF, to identify health sector savings and act on those findings.

Long term

- Increase current health spending in line with economic growth and increases in general government spending while also ensuring that in times of economic contraction, current levels of health spending are at least maintained in real per capita terms in order to realize the coverage and financial protection goals to which the government committed when it passed the Law on Financial Guarantees for Health Care Services.
- Ensure full commitment to current tax reform roadmaps, in particular, the tobacco tax roadmap, which envisions the gradual increase of tobacco rates in line with the EU-Ukraine Association Agreement as well as broader revenue administration reform.
- Consider introducing additional health taxes, such as for sugar, or further augmenting existing health taxes, such as on tobacco and alcohol, to increase overall fiscal revenues. These proceeds could potentially be earmarked for health, but careful consideration would need to be given to the trade-off of reduced budget flexibility.
- Regularly undertake whole-of-government spending reviews to reconsider functional priorities and accordingly adjust spending allocations across sectors.
- Increase spending efficiency through accelerated hospital rightsizing, especially in long-term TB care, gradual introduction of case-rate payments for inpatient care, and a clear strategy to promote a stronger role of PHC and integrated service provision.

- Prepare a long-term health financing strategy that can be politically endorsed and includes a vision for the expansion of the PMG and its financing, over a 10-year period, along with complementary visions for associated programs, such as the gradual expansion of the AMP to replace OOP spending on medicines and policies such as stronger rules to prevent overprescribing or health care quality improvement measures.

NOTES

1. As of 2017, this included 24 oblasts and the city of Kyiv, 148 cities (average population 130,000); 464 rayons (districts with an average population of 45,000); and 159 hromadas (communities with an average population of 9,000).
2. The ceilings for the PMG components (such as primary, specialized, or emergency care) are defined in the program passport approved by the Ministry of Health (MoH) with the consent of the Ministry of Finance (MoF); the NHSU/MoH, therefore, have significant within-year flexibility for changing the PMG expenditure composition.
3. Article 4 of the 2017 Law on Financial Guarantees for Health Care Services states population coverage as including "citizens, foreigners, stateless persons permanently residing in the territory of Ukraine, persons designated as refugees or persons in need of additional protection."
4. Data are from the Ukraine National Health Accounts 2018 and the State Statistics Service of Ukraine, http://www.ukrstat.gov.ua/
5. Data are from the World Bank World Development Indicators database.
6. Data are from the Ukraine National Health Accounts 2018 and the State Statistics Service of Ukraine.
7. The consolidated budget of Ukraine includes budgets of all government tiers. Namely, it includes the central budget and the subnational budgets.
8. In this report, the definition of "medical goods" corresponds to "Category HC.5 Medical goods" of the System of Health Accounts 2011 (https://www.oecd.org/publications/a-system-of-health-accounts-2011-9789264270985-en.htm), which covers pharmaceuticals (prescribed and over the counter); therapeutic appliances; and other medical goods such as glasses, hearing aids, orthopedic appliances, and medical durables including technical devices. In Ukraine's economic classification, this category of consumables is coded as 2220 "medicines and dressing supplies," which, despite the title, is not limited to pharmaceuticals but also includes therapeutic appliances and all kinds of medical goods (any medical equipment not classified as capital investment) (according to the MoF coding guidelines outlined in Section 2.2.2. of the MoF Order No. 333 of March 12, 2012, available at https://zakon.rada.gov.ua/laws/show/z0456-12#n16.
9. The range of OECD countries here is limited to those that have formally reported their levels of total pharmaceutical spending for both 2015 and 2018.
10. Data are sourced from the State Statistics Service of Ukraine.
11. Calculations are based on data collected by the State Statistics Service of Ukraine through the 2009–18 Household Living Condition Survey's module on self-perceived health status.
12. International comparisons are currently impossible because Ukraine collects the unmet need data by household rather than individual as in OECD countries.
13. Figure 2.4.4 shows the change in the shape of the concentration curves plotted for the two-period year moving average of the overall level of unmet need (measured as the share of households reporting such need). Each curve plots the cumulative percentage of the unmet health care need against the cumulative percentage of households ranked by income deciles. The blue curve depicts income distribution of the unmet need in 2009–10, and the red curve shows the situation as of 2017–18. During this decade, the curve moved closer to the full equality line. Illustrating that the concentration index, which measures the area between the concentration curve and the line of equality, grew from −0.15 to −0.12.

14. Calculations are based on data collected by the State Statistics Service of Ukraine through the 2009–18 Household Living Condition Survey's module on self-perceived health status.

15. OOP payments greater than 10 percent of total household consumption is the global metric used to monitor catastrophic health spending as part of the United Nations Sustainable Development Goal, Target 3.8 on Universal Health Coverage. Member states in the WHO European Region also monitor catastrophic spending using a "capacity to pay" approach, which is more sensitive to financial hardship among poorer households than the Sustainable Development Goal approach. Capacity to pay for health care is country-specific and measured as a household's total consumption minus a standard amount to cover basic needs such as food, housing, and utilities.

16. The framework law, "On State Financial Guarantees of Medical Services for the Population," November 2017 (amended twice in 2019) is located at https://zakon.rada.gov.ua/laws /show/2168-19.

17. The rules were issued in MoH Order #1709 of July 26, 2019. The full text is available at https://zakon.rada.gov.ua/laws/show/z0961-19.

18. "Emerging and development economies" are one of the two key groups in the IMF country classification, the other one being "advanced economies." According to the IMF, this classification is not based on strict criteria and evolves over time (http://datahelp.imf.org /knowledgebase/articles/778593-composition-of-current-statistical-groups-and-aggr). Within the emerging and development economies, countries are further classified into regional groupings: Asia, Europe, Latin America and the Caribbean, Middle East and Central Asia, and Sub-Saharan Africa. As of October 2020, the emerging and developing Europe group included 16 countries: Albania, Belarus, Bosnia and Herzegovina, Bulgaria, Croatia, Hungary, Kosovo, Moldova, Montenegro, North Macedonia, Poland, Romania, the Russian Federation, Serbia, Turkey, and Ukraine.

19. The respective IMF estimates of the consolidated deficit were not available at the time of preparing this report.

20. Data are from the World Bank World Development Indicators database.

21. Data are sourced from the MoH Centre of Medical Statistics, retrieved from http://medstat .gov.ua/ukr/main.html.

22. Dare are sourced from the World Bank World Development Indicators database.

23. Data are sourced from the MoH Centre of Medical Statistics and OECD statistics.

REFERENCES

IMF (International Monetary Fund). 2020. *World Economic Outlook: A Long and Difficult Ascent*. Washington, DC: IMF.

Ukraine Ministry of Health News. 2020. "П'ять пріоритетів Програми медичних гарантій" [Five priorities of the program of medical guarantees], January 15. Ministry of Health of Ukraine. https://moz.gov.ua/article/news/p%e2%80%99jat-prioritetiv-programi-medichnih -garantij.

World Bank. 2019. *Ukraine 2019 Public Expenditure and Financial Accountability Performance Assessment Report*. Washington DC: World Bank. https://openknowledge.worldbank.org /handle/10986/33626

3 Purchasing the Program of Medical Guarantees

WHAT IS COVERED BY THE PROGRAM OF MEDICAL GUARANTEES, AND HOW IS IT PURCHASED?

In 2020, the Program of Medical Guarantees (PMG) was expanded from covering only primary health care (PHC) services to all types of care, including hospital and specialized outpatient care. As discussed in chapter 2, the PMG is the benefit package that is guaranteed to be paid by public funds. In April 2020, in line with the original reform timeline, the scope of the PMG was expanded from PHC to cover the entire health care continuum, including PHC, specialized, and emergency care.

The National Health Service of Ukraine (NHSU) purchases PMG services through distinct service packages, developed on an annual basis, depending on the budget and health policy priorities. In 2020, all health care services in the PMG were initially organized into 27 packages of services. These were adjusted to include three additional packages for COVID-19-related health services plus a temporary package for hospitals that treated COVID-19 patients in the initial stages of the pandemic but were not designated as COVID-19 hospitals. Later in the year, a transformation package was added to support hospitals in adjusting to new contracting and provider payment methods. Service packages in PMG-2020, which was effective from April 2020 to March 2021, can be in general categorized into seven broad areas, as presented in figure 3.1. In late 2020, the PMG was organized into a primary care package, an emergency care package, 8 outpatient care packages, 12 hospital and complex care packages covering inpatient and outpatient care, 3 rehabilitation care packages, 2 palliative care packages, and 3 COVID-19 care packages (see figure 3.1). This approach was largely maintained in PMG-2021 covering May–December 2021, which was extended to 36 packages, mostly by unbundling some of the broader packages. It introduced separate packages for dental care and pregnancy management (previously part of the general outpatient care), a separate package for outpatient peritoneal hemodialysis (previously part of the general hemodialysis package), and a separate package for treatment of hematological diseases (previously part of general outpatient and inpatient care). PMG-2021 also included two entirely new outpatient care packages—support to tuberculosis (TB) patients at the primary care

FIGURE 3.1
Graphic presentation of the PMG components—PMG service packages

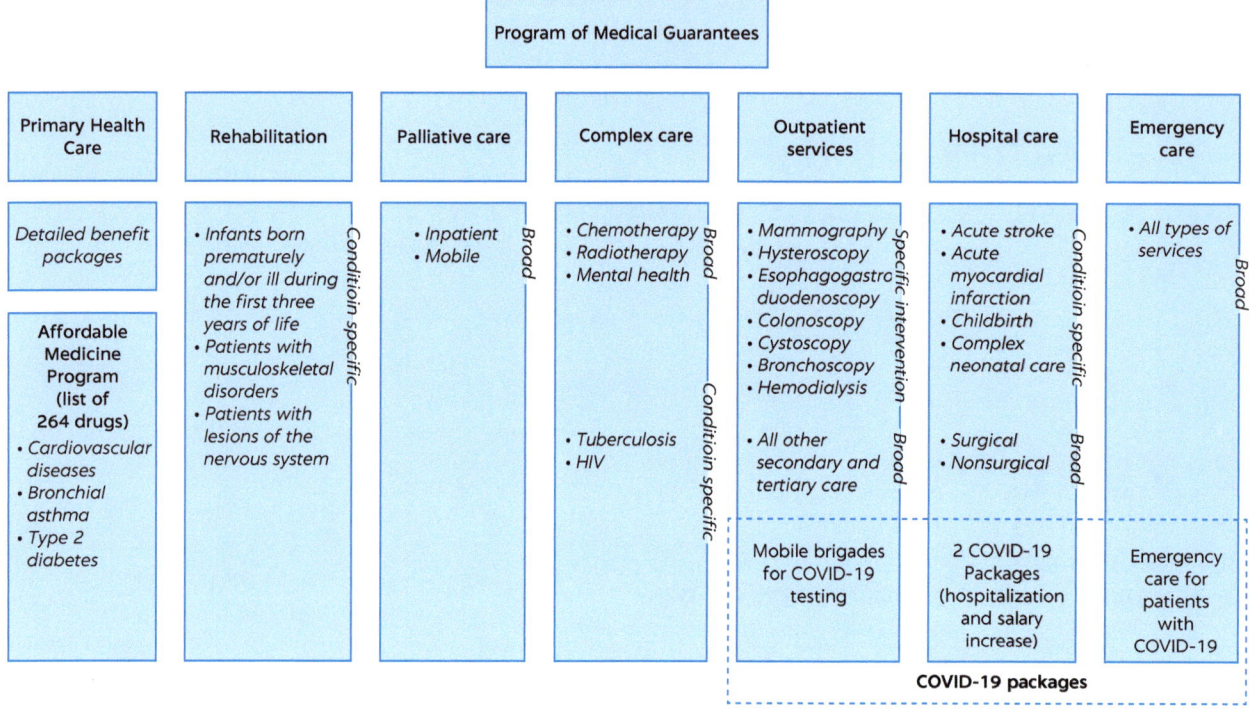

Source: World Bank.
Note: COVID-19 = coronavirus (pandemic).

level and psychiatric care by mobile interdisciplinary teams—and continued a range of COVID-19 related care, adding vaccinations. The transformation package was discontinued. The Affordable Medicines Program (AMP) (*Dostupni Liky*), which was part of the PMG-2020, is included in PMG-2021.

The NHSU purchases services from providers using contracts that define service specifications. Each package of care has specific requirements that providers must meet in order to contract with the NHSU. The service specifications are defined by the NHSU through working groups that include Ministry of Health (MoH) representatives, some international partners, service providers, and researchers. The specifications are mainly related to the organization of service provision, key equipment, and personnel of the providers. By defining service specifications, the NHSU is strengthening strategic purchasing. The use of specifications to define the eligibility of providers enables selective contracting of providers that can meet those standards with a view to efficiency and quality improvement.

Any provider can apply to provide any set of service packages—a practice that risks potential inequality in geographical access to services, with overconcentration in some areas and gaps in others. Purchasing rules for 2020 allowed any care provider to apply and sign a contract with the NHSU for one or more packages of service, subject to meeting the eligibility criteria. Contracting was not subject to a master plan for a network of services that would ensure a guaranteed health care supply. In other words, while the NHSU was able to use its contracting and purchasing power to improve the efficiency of contracted providers, it was not able to use contracting to strategically shape the provider network into a more efficient one. Moreover, contract requirements for specific types of equipment have prompted facilities to invest without the security that they would continue providing such services once the regional masterplans are crystalized.

Figure 3.2 presents the requirements that all contractors have to meet as well as the various service packages they can apply for.

Some packages are defined in more general terms, while others are condition-specific and more detailed. Looking across packages, it can be said that priority services tend to be defined more explicitly. These include acute stroke, acute myocardial infarction, childbirth, and complex neonatal care at the hospital level. A set of six diagnostic services, such as hemodialysis, is also organized into six individual service packages. As discussed elsewhere in this report, the process for defining these priorities is unclear. In contrast, *all* other types of outpatient specialized care are broadly defined as secondary and tertiary outpatient care and are aggregated into *one* package. A PHC package has its own definition and an explicit list of services covered at that level of care.

The NHSU purchases services from health care providers using different payment methods. The mix of payment methods used for contracting includes a global budget for the majority of hospital and specialized outpatient care as well as emergency medical services, case-based payments for inpatient priority services, fee-for-service for specific types of diagnostic examinations and types of treatment, and capitation for the PHC package, as shown in table 3.1. In addition, there are some other payments made to providers through the NHSU and financed as part of the PMG package. These payments relate to managing the financial risk associated with health financing reform and the COVID-19 pandemic. The first consists of compensatory lump-sum payments to facilities that experienced a substantial reduction in revenues following the April 2020 payment reform. The second is payments that have been in place since September 2020 to health personnel working in a subset of facilities and who have been paid temporary COVID-related salary top-ups equivalent to 70 percent top-ups for physicians, 50 percent for nurses, and 30 percent for junior medical staff.

In parallel with the rollout of the PMG, the government developed the e-Health system, which has been critical to the service-purchasing function. In April 2018, the government launched Ukraine's new national health information system, e-Health.[1] In the first years of reform (2018–19), e-Health was focused on supporting PMG payments for PHC—enrolling patients, contracting providers, and implementing and monitoring payments (see figure 3.3). It was also used to reimburse pharmacies for the AMP medicines. As the PMG expanded in 2020, the e-Health system was further developed to capture a larger set of providers, and electronic health records and e-Referrals were introduced. E-Health data are also pulled into extensive online dashboards, with PMG purchasing statistics on the NHSU website. Despite technical difficulties caused by, among other things, very tight reform deadlines, the e-Health system provides the NHSU with a wealth of basic PMG purchasing data that can be used not only for contract management and payment but also to monitor the services provided and inform decision-making and policy development in the sector.

In the remainder of this chapter, different types of care covered by the PMG will be discussed in more detail. Key recommendations for the expansion of the PMG package and the purchasing of services covered by the PMG are organized into the following sections: primary care, AMP, and specialized care—inpatient, outpatient, emergency, and hospital care.

FIGURE 3.2

Contracting requirements for the service packages under the NHSU

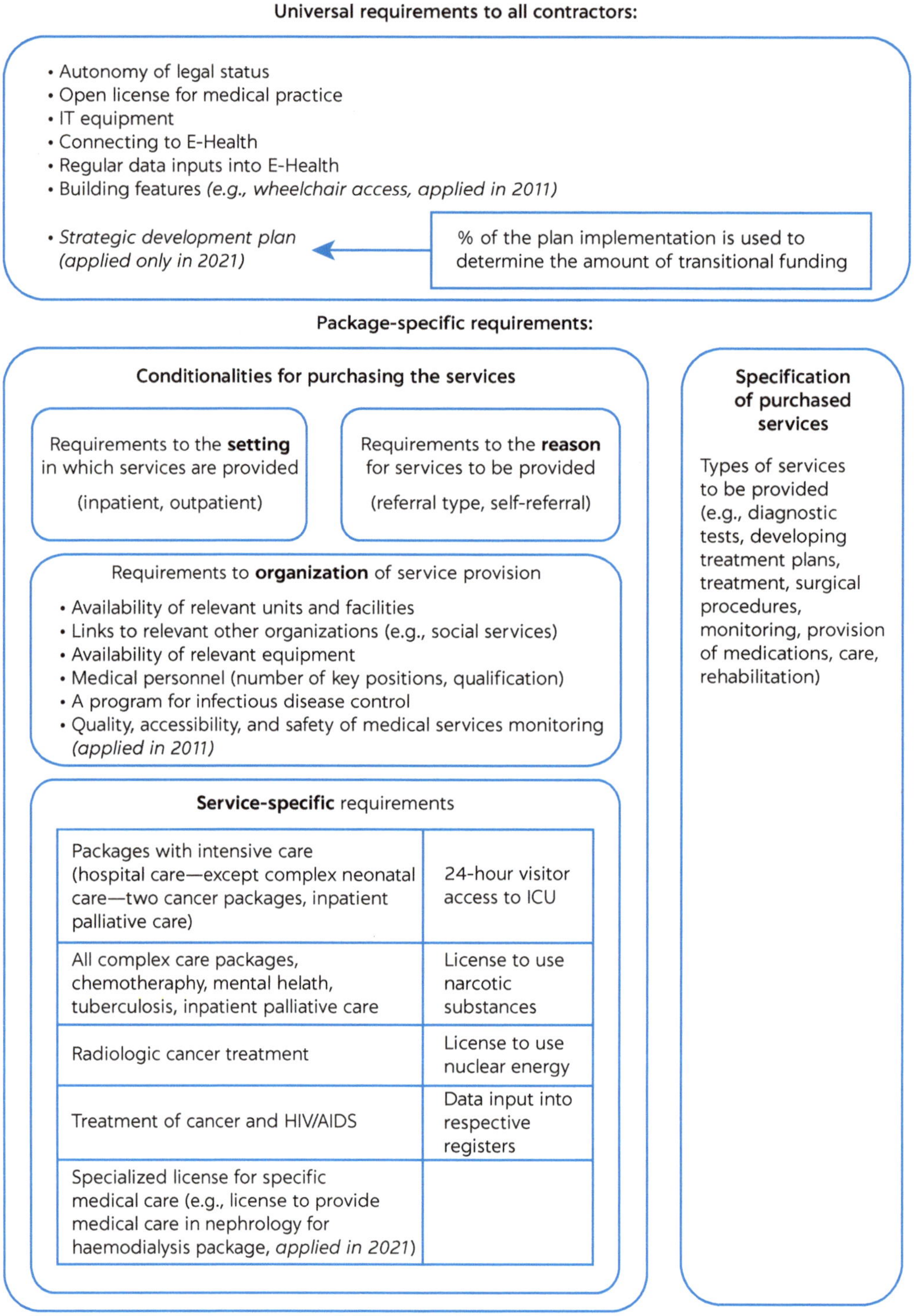

Universal requirements to all contractors:

- Autonomy of legal status
- Open license for medical practice
- IT equipment
- Connecting to E-Health
- Regular data inputs into E-Health
- Building features *(e.g., wheelchair access, applied in 2011)*

- *Strategic development plan (applied only in 2021)* ← % of the plan implementation is used to determine the amount of transitional funding

Package-specific requirements:

Conditionalities for purchasing the services

Requirements to the **setting** in which services are provided

(inpatient, outpatient)

Requirements to the **reason** for services to be provided

(referral type, self-referral)

Requirements to **organization** of service provision

- Availability of relevant units and facilities
- Links to relevant other organizations (e.g., social services)
- Availability of relevant equipment
- Medical personnel (number of key positions, qualification)
- A program for infectious disease control
- Quality, accessibility, and safety of medical services monitoring *(applied in 2011)*

Service-specific requirements

Packages with intensive care (hospital care—except complex neonatal care—two cancer packages, inpatient palliative care)	24-hour visitor access to ICU
All complex care packages, chemotheraphy, mental helath, tuberculosis, inpatient palliative care	License to use narcotic substances
Radiologic cancer treatment	License to use nuclear energy
Treatment of cancer and HIV/AIDS	Data input into respective registers
Specialized license for specific medical care (e.g., license to provide medical care in nephrology for haemodialysis package, *applied in 2021*)	

Specification of purchased services

Types of services to be provided (e.g., diagnostic tests, developing treatment plans, treatment, surgical procedures, monitoring, provision of medications, care, rehabilitation)

Source: Original figure for this publication based on analysis of NHSU package contracts.
Note: HIV/AIDS = human immunodeficiency virus/acquired immune deficiency syndrome; ICU = intensive care unit; IT = information technology.

TABLE 3.1 **Service packages of the PMG contracted by the NHSU in 2020**

TYPE OF CARE	NUMBER OF PACKAGES INCLUDED AND DESCRIPTION	PAYMENT METHODS	NUMBER OF PROVIDERS CONTRACTED		TOTAL VALUE OF CONTRACTS, UAH MILLIONS
			TOTAL	PRIVATE	
Primary care	1: Primary care	Age-adjusted capitation	1,695	588	16,022
Emergency care	2: Emergency care and COVID emergency care	Global budget	25	0	9,601
Hospital care					
Hospital priority packages	4: Acute stroke, acute myocardial infarction, childbirth, and complex neonatal care	Per case	537	2	4,782
COVID hospital packages	2: Special measures in April 2020 (a 300% salary top-up and additional medical supplies) and regular COVID care (including in-hospital COVID tests)	Global budget	366	0	7,655
Other hospital packages	2: Surgical and nonsurgical	Global budget	1,085	6	23,053
Outpatient care					
Select diagnostic procedures	7: Mammography, hysteroscopy, esophagogastro-duodenoscopy, colonoscopy, cystoscopy, bronchos-copy, hemodialysis	Fee-for-service	696	37	2,091
Mobile COVID brigades	1: Collection of samples for COVID testing by specialized mobile brigades	Global budget	938	3	655
Other types of outpatient care	1: Secondary and tertiary outpatient care	Global budget	1,429	34	6,637
Complex care (inpatient and outpatient)	6: Oncological packages, mental health, TB, HIV	Global budget	695	5	6,036
Rehabilitation	3: For infants born prematurely and/or ill during the first three years of life, for patients with musculo-skeletal disorders, for patients with lesions of the nervous system	Global budget	249	4	1,154
Palliative care	2: Inpatient and mobile	Global budget	485	1	513
Other payments (transitional financial support)					
Financial compensation for facilities losing revenues	Applied to facilities experiencing significant financial losses after the launch of hospital payments in April 2020	Per facility	490	0	1,930
Salary increase	Applied starting September 2020 to temporarily increase salaries of medical personnel during September–December 2020 (later extended to March 2021)	70% top-ups for physicians; 50% for nurses; 30% for junior medical staff	1,596	0	5,089
Total	31		**3,103**	**611**	**85,217**

Note: The totals do not add to 100 percent because of duplicates resulting from many providers contracted for delivery of multiple PMG packages. PMG = Program of Medical Guarantees.

PRIMARY CARE

The scope of the PMG package for primary care and modalities for purchasing PHC has not substantially changed since the launch of PHC reform in 2018. The benefit package for the primary care level was defined at the beginning of PMG implementation, and strategic purchasing of PHC services was the first step in the health financing reform. PHC services are explicitly defined under the PMG, and they are provided according to the established rule—for example,

FIGURE 3.3

E-Health development timeline

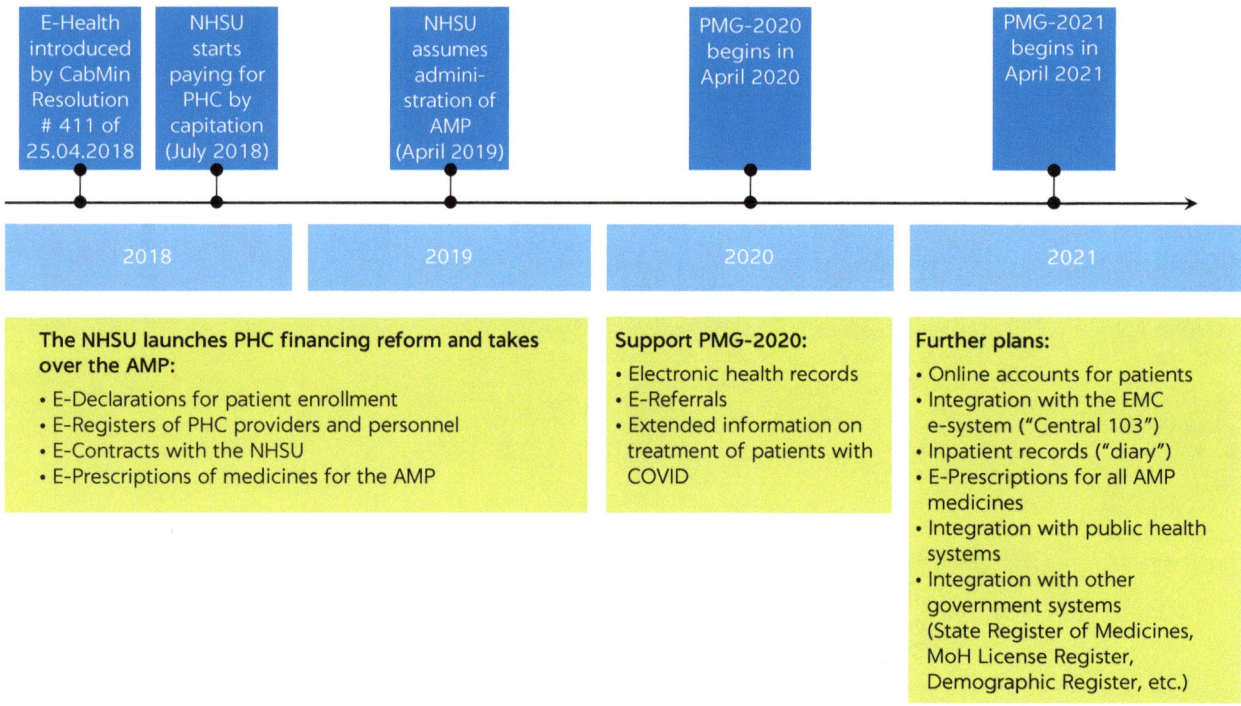

Source: Original figure for this publication.
Note: AMP = Affordable Medicines Program; EMC = emergency medical care; MoH = Ministry of Health; NHSU = National Health Service of Ukraine; PHC = primary health care.

registration with the PHC provider, paid by capitation, free of charge for the population, and no co-payments. Balance billing is not permitted. PHC providers may only charge patients for defined (chargeable) services listed in the Cabinet of Minister's Decree 1138[2] in an amount approved by local authorities. There have been no major changes to the definition of the PHC benefits package, purchasing arrangements, and service delivery requirements, except for an upward adjustment of capitation rates in November 2020 to compensate for the risks of delivering care during the COVID-19 pandemic and some COVID-related protocols to ensure health care worker and patient safety. As with all services in the PMG, utilities are paid by subnational governments (SNGs), and the SNGs can also add supplementary financing if they wish.

Scope of PHC services covered by the PMG

PHC services covered by the PMG are explicitly defined and provided to all residents of Ukraine enrolled with primary care physicians. These services include diagnostics and treatment of common and chronic conditions, preventive screening and vaccination, pregnancy, childcare, and certain types of emergency and palliative care. MoH Order 504 of 2018 defines the scope of PHC service, including 17 types of PHC consultations and interventions and 8 types of laboratory and diagnostic examinations as well as minimum requirements for staff and equipment.

The AMP, which pays for prescribed medicines purchased at pharmacies, is designed around the PHC benefit package. The PHC benefit package was designed in coordination with the design of the AMP— the program to fund the purchases of outpatient medications prescribed at the PHC level through reimbursement to contracted pharmacies. This program is discussed in detail in the section "AMP for Outpatient Care." The development of the AMP has proven to be a positive driver of PHC utilization. Most of the episodes of primary care registered in the electronic health record system during 2020 were related to patients seeking either referrals or drug prescriptions; over 60 percent of visits entailed prescriptions. Prescriptions were also quoted by PHC providers as one of the most frequent reasons for patient visits, along with management of chronic disease and issuance of sick leave notes.

MoH and NHSU started a gradual expansion of PHC services covered by PMG beginning in 2021. The expansion of PHC level benefits is intended to explicitly include services related to COVID-19, mental and behavioral disorders, additional laboratory tests, and services related to managing patients with chronic diseases, TB, and vaccination services not related to COVID.

Organization of PHC

Patients are required to enroll with a PHC provider on contract with the NHSU but can change their provider at any time. All citizens and permanent residents of Ukraine are given the right to choose a PHC physician, thereby enrolling with a PHC provider organization employing the doctor of their choice.[3] By April 2020, 24 months after enrollment began, 76 percent of the population (30.5 million people) had registered with a PHC provider.[4] Despite having the opportunity to change their chosen provider at any time, there has been no major migration of patients between providers since the beginning of the enrollment campaign; from January 2019–September 2020, the period for which data are available, only around 3.7 percent of the enrolled population had changed providers.[5]

Most PHC providers are PHC centers, which consolidate multiple doctors and service delivery locations under one legal entity; 23 percent are solo practices. In 2020, the NHSU contracted PMG services from 1,695 PHC providers. Of these, most (77 percent) were PHC centers (legal entities consisting of several PHC ambulatory facilities and operating as either communal not-for-profit organizations or private businesses) and the rest (23 percent) were private solo practices.[6] Overall, 35 percent of all the providers were privately owned. Most of the doctors working in these facilities are family physicians (66 percent), with the rest being pediatricians (20 percent) and therapists (15 percent). No data are available on mid-level personnel.

The average number of patients per physician is broadly within the recommended limit and almost the same in rural and urban areas. Providers are recommended to keep enrollment within the limit of 1,800 per family doctor, 2,000 adults per therapist, and 900 children per pediatrician. Average enrollment numbers have stayed within this limit (with an average PHC provider having 1,300 patients per one physician, including 1,465 patients per family physician, 1,336 per therapist, and 713 per pediatrician), but around 8 percent of the practices have exceeded the recommended threshold. Half of the providers operate in rural areas. They are typically smaller compared to those in the cities: an average rural PHC provider has 1,754 patients per practice (one location) compared to 7,453 patients in big cities and 5,462 in smaller towns. At the same time, the average number of patients per one physician is almost the same in rural and urban areas.

Quality of care is not yet systematically measured and assessed at either the provider or the system level. The NHSU monitors PHC providers for contractual compliance and potential fraud, but there is no monitoring of performance or quality improvement, nor are there clinical audit measures. The e-Health system helps the NHSU monitor compliance with contract conditionalities and minimize potential fraud. However, there is currently no system in place to measure and improve quality. PHC clinical guidelines are not regularly updated, and while the MoH has provided physicians with access to over 1,000 Duodecim, evidence-based guidelines licensed from the Finnish Medical Society, only a few have been translated from English, and they have not been adapted to the Ukrainian context. For instance, the guidelines reference medicines and treatments that are currently not part of the Essential Medicines List (EML). Also, the use of the Finnish guidelines is optional. The NHSU intended to introduce contract conditionalities related to performance, focusing on preventive activities, risk group screening, and access to outpatient medicines for target groups of patients with chronic conditions. Starting in September 2021, a top-up performance payment was introduced for the vaccination of children up to age 6 years against measles.

Existing regulations do not yet clearly define the PHC service delivery model and how it should be integrated with other levels of care. PHC delivery is regulated by a range of MoH orders[7] that allow various care organization options but do not provide guidance on PHC objectives, PHC's role in the wider health system, and desirable delivery models. The MoH has started preparing documents to fill this gap—for example, the "White Paper on Health Service Delivery Model in Ukraine" (WHO and Ministry of Health of Ukraine 2020) and the draft "Concept of Primary Health Care Development in Ukraine to 2031" currently being prepared by the Ministry of Health of Ukraine (Ministry of Health of Ukraine, n.d.), but none have yet been formally approved. Current proposals for a new vision for primary care include a move to a group practice model with an expanded skill mix and multidisciplinary teams; a greater role for the prevention and management of noncommunicable diseases (NCDs), including mental health and infectious diseases such as TB; a wider range of care services; and a new quality improvement system. Other changes, such as expanding the role of nursing staff, have been discussed but have not yet been taken up.

The use of digital technologies in the provision of PHC is not yet well developed in Ukraine. While basic equipment and technologies to support e-Health —computers, an internet connection, and a management information system— are contract requirements and therefore all PHC facilities have them, digital technologies are not yet used to their full potential. Indeed, a 2019 survey of PHC providers in remote areas found that over 90 percent had permanent access to the internet and a personal computer for providing services online (Ministry of Health of Ukraine 2019). Over the past decade, Ukraine has attempted to strengthen the use of digital technologies, often referred to as telemedicine,[8] in PHC provisions through several pilot-level initiatives. In 2017, the law "On Improved Access and Quality of Health Care in Rural Areas"[9] introduced the concept of telemedicine and listed a wide range of equipment and infrastructure that could be purchased from the central budget to enable wider utilization of digital technologies in the delivery of the PMG. However, a coherent strategy for implementing telemedicine in Ukraine has not yet been developed, and its potential remains unrealized.

The COVID-19 pandemic has posed challenges to PHC service organization and provision, but it also hastened some needed changes, including the adoption and use of digital technologies for consultations. Generally, PHC providers reported pressure related to the provision of care and follow-up with patients with suspected or confirmed COVID-19. But COVID-19 also prompted some positive adjustments and accelerated needed changes to service organization. For example, it has shown how critical teleconsultations can be to the delivery of essential services and reinforced the need to design an actionable plan for developing digital health in Ukraine, including ways to ensure access to technology, adoption of relevant tools and skills, and privacy protection. To address changes needed to service organization and provision, the MoH together with the NHSU, development partners, and selected representatives of PHC providers, established a working group and prepared revised standards of care and service organization for COVID-19.

Payment for primary care through the PMG by capitation

PHC providers are paid based on a national capitation rate, adjusted for age and geographic terrain. In the first 6 months after the reform was launched (July–December 2018), the PHC providers contracted by the NHSU received a simple capitation budget based on actual enrollment. A unified capitated rate is set at the national level and adjusted by age (0–5, 6–17, 18–39, 40–64, 65 years and older) and geographic terrain to account for the higher cost of provision in mountainous areas. The capitation budget covers wages, medicines, supplies, and administrative costs. From 2019 onward, the NHSU introduced a formula adjustment to penalize providers that exceed the recommended number of enrolled individuals: the capitation rate is decreased[10] if the provider exceeds the limit by 10 percent and is set to zero for any patients enrolled above 150 percent of the recommended capacity.

Payments are not adjusted to account for differences in group and solo practices. There are no financial incentives to build a group practice or to form a network to share some resources such as labs, diagnostics, managerial/administrative functions, and staff. There are also no built-in incentives for a provider to expand the PHC team into a more multidisciplinary practice. However, PHC providers do have the flexibility to add specialists, such as social workers, to their team.

The base capitation rate was increased by 8.5 percent from November 2020 and remained at this level in the PMG-2021 to reflect the growing COVID-19 workload, including collecting test samples. The COVID-19–related expansion of the PMG in April 2020 included a new package for health providers, including PHC providers, to set up mobile teams for collecting testing samples. This package was expected to cover, among other costs, a 300 percent top-up on the salaries of health workers in the mobile team but not the costs of the actual test, which was funded separately. By December 2020, only 33 percent of all PHC providers contracted with the NHSU—556 out of 1,681[11]—had signed up for this package; eligibility included collecting at least 150 testing samples a month, and COVID-19 testing was not included in the list of services that PHC providers were manded to provide.[12] However, providers had the option of referring patients for testing in other facilities since testing was not included. Beginning in November 2020, MoH included COVID-19 test sample collection on the list of mandatory services for PHC providers. To compensate for this change and other costs of the growing COVID-19 workload, such as observation of patients treated at home, the government increased the PHC base capitation rate by 8.5 percent, also from November 2020. An increased base capitation rate, but no extra package for mobile teams, was maintained in the PMG-2021 through December 2021. The package paying for mobile testing teams was discontinued in January 2021.

Also, in the PMG-2021, the NHSU extended the PHC financing model to include the capitation mechanism and additional financial incentives through a pay-for-performance top-up. Paying for health care by capitation is a simple and effective way to discourage excessive billing for services, but it also entails the potential risk that doctors may provide less care than is needed by the patients. For example, once doctors enroll a patient and secure the corresponding capitation amount, they may spend less time on consultations and perform fewer diagnostic procedures than needed. To some extent, this risk is mitigated by Ukraine's approach of enabling patients to change PHC providers, which incentivizes quality through competition. However, this is not always sufficient, especially if the choice of providers is limited, such as in rural areas. Combining capitation with other payment mechanisms, such as payment for performance, may help offset these perverse incentives and better ensure quality. The NHSU is developing a range of innovations to this end, some of which are already included in the PMG-2021. These include a pay-for-performance element for the attainment of immunization coverage goals and per-patient payments to support outpatient treatment of patients with TB at the PHC level in coordination with a TB specialist at a higher level of care. Moreover, the new PMG-2021 package covering COVID vaccinations will have a pay-for-performance element to reward each vaccination conducted by the contracted provider. Detection and management of NCDs is another area that has a high potential for introducing a pay-for-performance element, but there are currently no plans for this.

Recommendations

The PMG reforms of 2017–20 gave a significant boost to PHC by raising the overall level of financing, introducing new payment methods that incentivize delivery of care, giving providers more autonomy and flexibility, and expanding the use of electronic health systems. Overall, the PHC component of health financing reform is well designed and well implemented. For PHC to realize its potential for improving population health outcomes, additional measures are needed, described in the sections that follow:

Short term

- Finalize and approve a strategic vision for PHC service delivery, ideally as a part of a broader health service delivery model covering the entire health care continuum. This would create the opportunity for PHC to take on new functions and to coordinate with specialized, emergency, palliative, and public health care to tackle diseases at an earlier stage, thus lowering the overall cost of care in Ukraine.
- Develop policies and functions in the MoH and NHSU to systematically measure and assess the quality of care. Introduce a performance monitoring framework for PHC to benchmark performance across facilities and within facilities across time and improve accountability for the delivery of quality care.

- Promote and strengthen the use of digital technologies to significantly enhance access to and the quality of PHC. Expansion of teleconsultations would help provide better service to patients living in remote areas, the elderly, and those with mobility challenges, and also help maintain essential services during subsequent waves of the COVID-19 pandemic and any future pandemics. In addition to the already existing basic regulations, the government needs a more comprehensive strategy and a realistic action plan to ensure the needed investment, rules, and skills are addressed.
- Consider expanding the use of performance-based payments that are complementary to capitation to encourage PHC providers to actively reach out to people in need of services and improve data collection on PHC performance. This could be one of the first steps to help strengthen the management of major chronic diseases and to stimulate the provision of certain services such as TB and immunization, which may be underprovided. It would also provide data on key areas of PHC performance.

Long term

- Review the contracting criteria applied by the NHSU to promote the newly formalized service delivery vision for PHC to increase and align the capacity to address the existing disease burden and strengthen resilience to new challenges such as epidemics.
- Introduce standardized clinical protocols mandated for use within the PMG at the primary care level. This will not only help ensure clinical care quality but will also guide providers on the most cost-effective care that they can provide within their capitation budget.
- Develop a process for planned, regular revision of the capitation rate to consider any increases in input costs (for example, inflation, salary increases) and changes in the scope of services in the PHC package, supported by robust costing methodologies.
- Develop mechanisms for interterritorial (interhromada) cooperation among groups of neighboring hromadas to support sharing resources among small, rural PHC centers.

THE AMP FOR OUTPATIENT CARE

Scope of the AMP

The AMP was introduced in 2017 to increase the availability and affordability of outpatient medicines through contracted pharmacies for patients with high-priority conditions. Originally, it was administered by SNGs and funded with an earmarked grant from the national government. The NHSU assumed the administration of the AMP in 2019, first as a standalone program and then as one of the components within the PMG. Initially, the AMP covered three selected conditions: cardiovascular diseases (CVDs), bronchial asthma (BA), and Type 2 diabetes (DM-2). The list of medicines covered by the AMP has been gradually expanding; it currently includes 27 international nonproprietary names (INNs) and 297 medicines[13] but remains focused on the three initial conditions identified as high priority.

The list of eligible medicines in the AMP is defined based on INNs and then specified by brands through a call to willing brand holders whose medicines are included in the national EML. To identify medicines eligible for reimbursement under the AMP, the government approves a list of INNs, none of which are attached to particular brands. Pharmaceutical trademark owners or their representatives can then apply to have their products included as candidates for reimbursement, provided that their medicines are also included in Ukraine's EML (approved by the Cabinet of Ministers [CabMin]). If their applications are successful, their medicines are then included on the "register of medicines eligible for reimbursement," which is revised twice a year. Ad hoc revisions are also allowed in cases when the government changes the internationally referenced price limits applied to the national EML. However, the EML is outdated as it includes medicines that do not correspond to modern clinical guidelines as well as monotherapies rather than combination therapies that are preferred by doctors and patients.

Despite some progress toward introducing health technology assessments (HTAs), no regulation defines clear rules and criteria for including and excluding medicines (INNs) on the EML, which would then inform the list of AMP medicines. In December 2020, the government approved guidelines for performing HTAs[14] that were expected to be introduced for medicines immediately and include nonpharmaceutical medical technologies from January 1, 2022. The HTA would be performed by a newly created state enterprise, and until the enterprise is established, this function would be temporarily performed by the existing state enterprise, the "State Expert Center," which operates under the MoH with the general function of state pharmaceutical control. However, detailed rules for performing an HTA for medicines are still to be developed by the MoH.

In 2021, the NHSU extended AMP coverage to include additional medicines for CVDs as well as medicines for outpatient treatment of neurological disease and mental health conditions (from October) and insulin (from July). The NHSU extended the AMP by including 3 more INNs for heart attack and stroke secondary prevention and 10 INNs for treatment of neurological diseases and mental health conditions—psychiatric conditions, anxiety, and depression. However, unlike the medicines for CVDs, BA, and DM-2, which are provided based on prescription by a PHC provider, medicines to treat neurological diseases and mental health conditions will have to be prescribed by neurologists and psychiatrists.

Beginning October 2021, the inclusion of funding for the provision of insulin to patients with diabetes has a slightly different scheme for prescription and reimbursement. Before 2017, insulin treatment for patients with diabetes was funded by SNGs as part of their broad health care responsibility. In 2017, the government launched a pilot project to test a reimbursement payment mechanism for the purchase of insulin, but it was still administered through the SNGs and funded through a health grant from the MoH, with supplementation from local revenue.

The number of pharmacies contracted by the NHSU for the AMP and the number of patients covered by the AMP continues to grow, although the number of prescriptions filled dropped significantly with the spread of the COVID pandemic. Since the transfer of the AMP program to the NHSU in April 2019, the number of patients using the program has grown from 0.3 million to just over 2.5 million in December 2020, as presented in figure 3.4.

FIGURE 3.4

Cumulative number of patients in the AMP

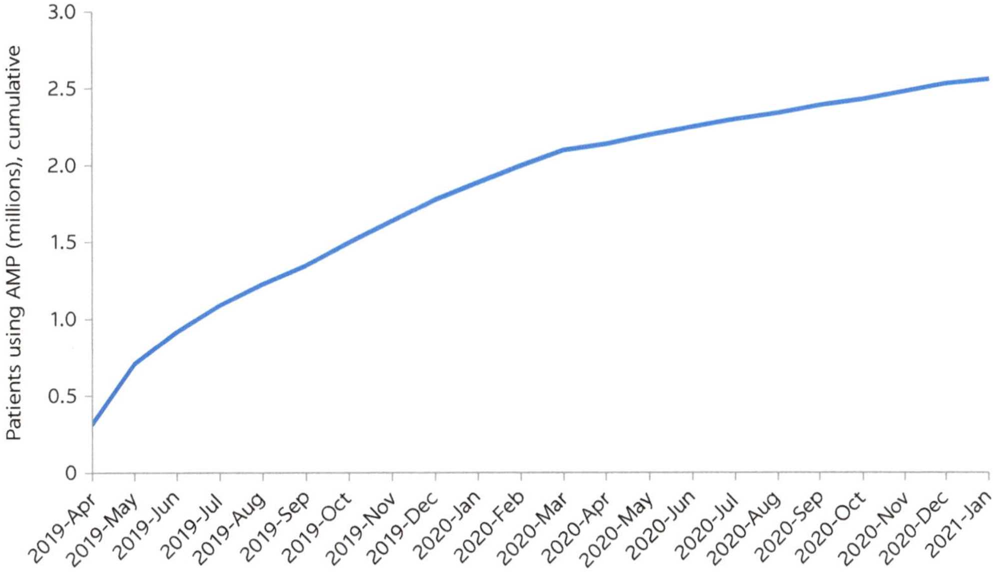

Source: NHSU dashboard, https://edata.e-health.gov.ua/e-data/dashboard.
Note: AMP = Affordable Medicines Program.

The NHSU estimated that by the end of 2020, extending the scope of the AMP helped cover 57 percent of all patients with BA, 44 percent patients with DM-2, and 18 percent of all patients with CVDs. There are currently 9,295 pharmacies or drug-dispensing points (operating under 1,136 legal entities participating in the AMP as of March 2021). Equity in access to benefits of the AMP remains a challenge and should be further improved, especially geographical equity. While all oblasts saw increases in the number of AMP-contracted pharmacies between 2019 and 2021, coverage across oblasts ranges from 17 to 30 pharmacies per 100,000 population, as figure 3.5 shows.

Despite the growing number of participants, the monthly number of reimbursed prescriptions was lower throughout most of 2020 compared to the same months of 2019, especially October through December (figure 3.6). During November 2020, the gap with the previous year was around 300,000 prescriptions, down by almost a quarter. This probably reflects decreased utilization of primary care since the beginning of the COVID-19 pandemic and therefore the inability to get prescriptions financed by the AMP.

AMP payment mechanism

To enter into a reimbursement agreement with the NHSU, the pharmacy must meet predefined requirements, including a valid license to retail medicines; information technology capabilities to support the Pharmacy Information System (AIC), which allows information to be exchanged with a central e-Health database; and qualified electronic signatures of all employees who will dispense medicines by electronic prescription.

The NHSU reimburses contracted pharmacies for prescribed medicines purchased using the e-Prescription part of the e-Health system. Patients with CVDs, BA, and DM-2 receive prescriptions from their family doctors and obtain the

FIGURE 3.5

Number of pharmacies that participated in the AMP per 100,000 population

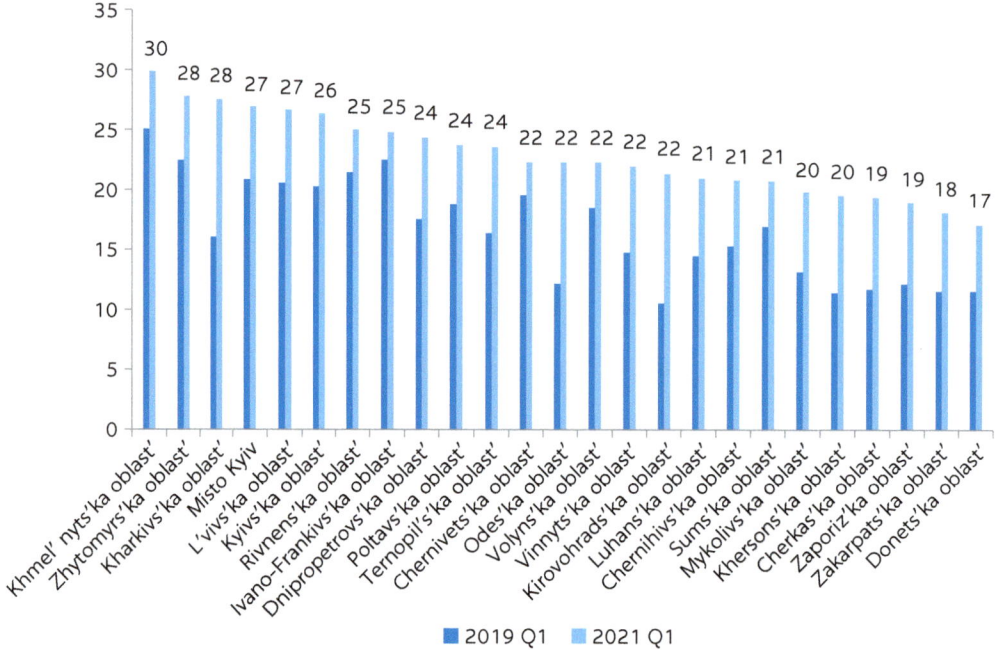

Source: NHSU dashboard, https://edata.e-health.gov.ua/e-data/dashboard.

FIGURE 3.6

Monthly number of AMP prescriptions

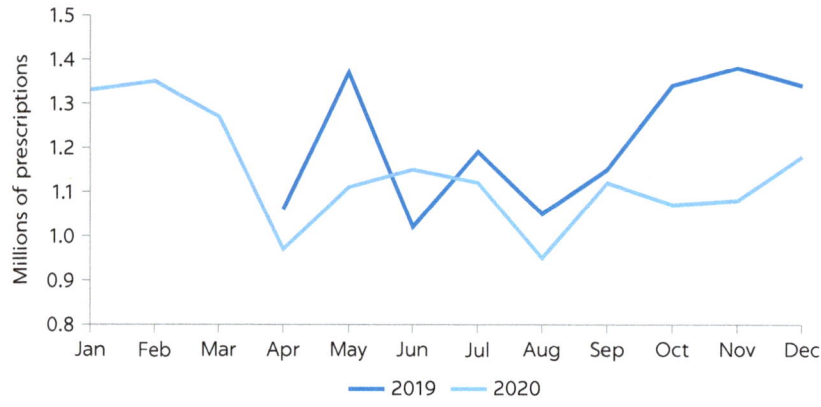

Source: NHSU dashboard, https://edata.e-health.gov.ua/e-data/dashboard.

prescribed medicines free of charge or with a small co-payment at NHSU-contracted pharmacies. The entire process—patient identification, medicine prescription, medicine provision, verification, and reimbursement—is supported by the e-Health system's e-Prescription. The e-Health system is also used for internal verification of reimbursement claims and also generates a vast range of data, some of which is published online and on live dashboards. The dashboards include information on pharmacies contracted under the AMP by geographic area, detailed information on prescribed and dispensed medicines, and reimbursement. The e-Prescription system is currently limited to prescriptions for medicines in the AMP program, with all other prescriptions remaining paper-based.

Reimbursement *prices* are set by the MoH based on a combination of domestic and international price referencing. Reimbursement *policy* is set by the MoH, using a combination of international and domestic price referencing. Data from five Eastern European countries—the Czech Republic, Hungary, Latvia, Poland, and the Slovak Republic—are used to define a median reference price for each INN. Brand-name generics in the local market that are priced above the reference (international) price are not reimbursed. For each reimbursed INN, the cheapest brand-name generic price in the local market becomes the reimbursement reference tariff. Brand-name generics in the local market that are priced below the reimbursement (international) price, but above the reimbursement reference tariff (domestic), are reimbursed, but the patient pays the difference between the market price and the reimbursement reference tariff. This means that the patient can obtain medicine free of charge, if he or she is willing to take the cheapest generic. This approach to price-setting makes medicines more affordable for patients, but it does not guarantee that patients have access to the cheapest alternative.

The AMP budget is defined based on trends in coverage, the expected number of patients and prescriptions by disease groups, and monthly spending limits defined at the NHSU level, after which the issuance of e-Prescriptions eligible for reimbursement are halted until the following month. The NHSU has been gradually refining its approach to AMP budget planning. Initially, the AMP spending projection was based solely on the number of prescriptions. Starting from 2020, the NHSU uses an estimated number of patients and needs by disease category as a basis for budget planning and reporting.[15] This approach became possible with the help of the E-Health system, which helps to identify the number of unique patients using the AMP, seasonal differences in utilization, and co-morbidity patterns. The e-Health system monitors the combined monthly cost of all registered prescriptions against the monthly spending limit. According to the legislation, once the monthly cost of the issued prescription exceeds the limit, issuance of any further e-Prescriptions for reimbursed medicines is halted until the next month. At that point, patients can buy these medicines at pharmacies at full price but without reimbursement. In practice, however, there has never been a situation where the NHSU exceeded the monthly AMP budget limits.

Recommendations

The AMP plays an important role in providing the population with free or low-cost medicines for conditions that affect a large share of the population and can be effectively managed with the right medication. Still, there are important measures that can be taken to improve its clinical appropriateness, cost-effectiveness, and equity:

Short term

- Update the EML on which the AMP draws and ensure that the medicines included are aligned with modern clinical guidelines and are cost-effective. In addition, to ensure timely updates of the EML in the future, the regulations governing the new HTA process (which will be used to update the EML) need to be finalized (according to the schedule established by CabMin Resolution in December 2020).

- Assess the trade-off between including more conditions and medicines in the AMP (some potentially expensive) and the scope, sufficient funding, and ability to provide other less costly and cost-effective medicines that address conditions afflicting a large number of people. Assess the effect on the PMG as well. HTA can also play a role in this.
- Ensure that as the AMP expands, it does so equitably across the regions and different socioeconomic areas within each region to rectify the country's geographic imbalances in its population's access to AMP-contracted pharmacies. The NHSU and MoH way wish to actively approach pharmacies in underserved areas for potential contracting.

Long term

- Explore the potential for the NHSU to play a role in monitoring prescribing behavior not only for potential fraud by providers or patients but also to improve the clinical quality of care through assessing whether prescriptions are needed and suitable for the diagnosed condition.

- Consider gradually extending the e-Prescription system to cover the full range of prescriptions, including those that are not part of the AMP. This would enable stronger control of prescriptions to address misuse, fraud, and overprescription, and ensure clinical appropriateness.

SPECIALIZED CARE: INPATIENT, OUTPATIENT, EMERGENCY, AND HOSPITAL CARE

Specialized care, a new component of the PMG package added in April 2020, has been modified repeatedly to address the need for COVID-related care and mitigate risk and financial losses associated both with COVID-19 and health financing reform. Starting from April 2020, the government expanded the PMG, which previously was limited to PHC services, to also include all types of specialized care—inpatient, outpatient, and emergency care. The NHSU started purchasing these services using a mix of new payment methods, which were expected to significantly redistribute historical financing across providers, with some hospitals benefiting and others experiencing significant losses. Simultaneously, uneven changes in SNG support for municipal hospitals compounded financial risk and, in some cases, aggravated losses. To compensate providers for the potential revenue shortfall, the government introduced a transitional PMG component providing financial support to these hospitals to cap losses at 10 percent of previous budgets.[16] This stage of the reform coincided with the beginning of the COVID-19 pandemic, complicating the implementation of the reform and necessitating adjustments. In particular, the government introduced additional service packages for providers treating COVID-19 patients and expanded transitional support to compensate hospitals for the revenue losses resulting from forgone care during the pandemic.

Organization of specialized care

Inpatient care in Ukraine is provided by an extensive and arguably excessive network of hospitals. While hospitalization rates for curative care are similar to

EU13 neighbors, the average length of stay (ALOS) is substantially higher than in EU13 countries (10.33 days versus 6.6. days),[17] which means that even though bed density is also considerably higher than the EU13 average (5.51 per 1,000 population versus 4.26 per 1,000 population),[18] the bed occupancy rate is around 85 percent (which is much higher than EU member states, where it ranges from 65 percent to 82 percent).[19] The hospital-centric character of service delivery persists despite a noticeable decline in hospitalization rates, ALOS, and bed density since 2015, owing to hospital rightsizing initiatives of the government that cut beds and, in some cases, also facilities. There is room for further rightsizing, though.

In contrast to European countries, Ukraine maintains a segregated system of disease-specific hospitals providing long-term inpatient care. The number of beds for TB patients is particularly excessive: of the total hospital beds in Ukraine, 4.1 percent are used to treat TB patients; ALOS for those beds is 85.6 days (in 2019),[20] because patients stay beyond the intensive care period and might not even have active TB. Ukraine also maintains a large network of psychiatric hospitals, reflecting the legacy of highly institutionalized care for mental health: 11.4 percent of all hospital beds are for psychiatric or neurological care, with ALOS averaging 35.2 days (50.6 days for adults).[21] While bed density in psychiatric hospitals has declined moderately as a result of rightsizing, hospitalization rates for mental health have remained unchanged and psychiatric hospitals continue to operate at 92 percent capacity.[22] In addition to the TB and psychiatric hospitals, there are highly specialized inpatient care facilities and dispensaries focusing on cancer, cardiological diseases, infectious diseases, human immunodeficiency virus / acquired immune deficiency syndrome (HIV/AIDS), and rare diseases.

Most hospital beds in the country (92.2 percent) are under the MoH, but the share of beds belonging to the security and defense sector and the private sector has been growing since 2015.[23] This can also be seen in health workforce numbers, where the share of health care professionals in private medical employment grew from 4.5 percent in 2014 to 7.6 percent in 2019.[24]

Specialized outpatient care is delivered by outpatient units in hospitals, clinical-diagnostic centers (reformed former polyclinics), or private solo practices. In principle, physical proximity of multidisciplinary specialists in PHC centers or clinical-diagnostic centers should facilitate better coordination between PHC and specialized outpatient services and even shift outpatient care out of hospitals. However, joint location is far from sufficient to ensure coordinated care, which also needs to be supported by new skills and the appropriate incentives at all levels of care.

Early in 2020, as part of the reforms toward enhancing efficiency in the hospital service delivery network, the government approved a list of 212 "hub hospitals" to constitute the network of providers ("capable network") to be developed in the future. This plan represents an important step toward having a more rational and efficient approach to investment in the hospital sector. However, significant discretion in the selection of the hospitals, despite criteria having been set, raises questions as to whether this list of hospitals is optimal.

The reform of the health service delivery model is being guided by a range of separate strategies, but there is no overarching, integrated concept to ensure alignment across types of care. There is a draft "White Paper on Health Service Delivery in Ukraine" (WHO and Ministry of Health of Ukraine 2020) that envisages an integrated model of service delivery across all types of care, but no formal strategy to this end has been adopted or even developed.

Scope of specialized care covered by the PMG

In April 2020, for the first time, Ukraine introduced a benefit package for specialized care. The PMG specified the services to be covered in inpatient and outpatient settings as well as a range of services for prehospital emergency medical care (EMC) treatment and mobile care. Before this, specialized care was financed using an input-based approach, in other words through approving facility budget requests organized by economic line items, such as salaries and utilities.

Figure 3.7 details the specialized care services within the PMG, which are divided into 25 service packages, each contracted separately. They include four COVID-19 packages that were added in response to the pandemic and four broad packages covering the rest of care. Sixteen packages are defined as conditions and cover a comprehensive set of services to treat them, such as acute stroke, childbirth, mental health, TB, HIV, and COVID-19. A further nine packages are defined as service inputs, which can be used to treat a variety of conditions, such as colonoscopy, hemodialysis, and radiotherapy, for example. All other services that did not fall into any of these groups were covered by the remaining four broad packages defined by provider setting—inpatient, outpatient, and emergency care—and also paid through the PMG. Specifically, figure 3.7 illustrates the following:

- Comprehensive sets of services to treat specific conditions. Of the 25 service packages, 16 were defined based on the treated condition.

FIGURE 3.7

Packages of specialized care in the PMG, 2020

Specific conditions		Specific interventions / specific services		Broad specification by type of provider setting	
Inpatient (4)	• Acute stroke • Acute myocardial infarction • Childbirth • Complex neonatal care	Outpatient (7)	• Mammography • Hysteroscopy • Esophagogastroduodeno scopy • Colonoscopy • Bronchoscopy • Cystoscopy • Hemodialysis	Outpatient (1)	• All other types of outpatient care
Complex care (3)	• Mental health • Tuberculosis • HIV			Inpatient (2)	• All other types of surgical inpatient care • All other types of nonsurgical inpatient care
Rehabilitation (3)	• Infants born prematurely and/or ill during 1–3 years of life • Musculoskeletal disorders • Lesions of the nervous system	Complex care (2)	• Chemotherapy • Radiotherapy	Emergency care (1)	• All types of emergency care
Palliative (2)	• Inpatient care • Mobile care				
COVID (4)	• Mobile testing brigades • Emergency care • Hospitalization • Transitional financing				
+16		**+9**		**+4 = 29**	

Source: Prepared by World Bank staff using data from the NHSU, accessible at https://contracting.nszu.gov.ua/.

This included: (1) four explicitly defined packages of inpatient care conditions—acute stroke, acute myocardial infarction, childbirth, and complex neonatal care; (2) three types of complex care packages to treat mental health, TB, and HIV; (3) three for rehabilitation care; (4) two palliative care packages; and (5) four packages to treat COVID-19 patients. Some of the packages in this group, such as rehabilitation, are more narrowly defined; others are more broadly defined. For example, treatment for TB patients includes inpatient and outpatient modalities as well as drug-sensitive and drug-resistant TB.

- Specific services or interventions. PMG-2020 included seven outpatient care packages, each covering one specific diagnostic or treatment service—mammography, hysteroscopy, esophagogastroduodenoscopy, colonoscopy, bronchoscopy, cystoscopy, and hemodialysis. The objective of putting specific outpatient services into separate packages was to stimulate the provision of such services by providers, including at the outpatient level. It was also intended to encourage private providers to contract with the NHSU to deliver these services financed by the PMG. In addition, PMG-2020 included two complex care packages for chemotherapy and radiotherapy.

- Broadly specified packages of outpatient, inpatient, and emergency care. All other services not falling under the separately specified packages are purchased in four broad packages defined by the provider setting. The packages include one bulk package for outpatient care, two broad packages for acute inpatient hospital care (surgical and nonsurgical), and an emergency EMC package. The very broad specification of these large packages entails a substantial risk of implicit service rationing by providers and obfuscates the role of the NHSU as a strategic service purchaser. While the two inpatient care packages are defined without specification by individual services, hospitals delivering such packages are required to report to the NHSU by cases categorized into a set of diagnosis-related groups (DRGs) developed by Ukraine and based on the Australian Refined DRG system. Overall, the two hospital care packages include 131 groups as defined by Ukrainian DRGs (UDRGs). Specification of the EMC package limits emergency services to cases of life-threatening conditions but also includes EMC phone counseling and disaster response.

Not shown in figure 3.7 are the additional payments to hospitals to cover losses from transition to the new payment mechanism and COVID-related salary increases that were processed as separate "packages" of the PMG. The additional service packages purchased to address the COVID-19 pandemic included collecting samples for laboratory testing of patients with COVID-19 symptoms, emergency transportation, hospital care, and transitional financial support. To respond to the COVID-19 pandemic, the PMG was expanded to cover additional services provided to people affected by COVID-19. In May 2020, 237 hospitals were contracted to provide COVID-19 care (including testing), 127 mobile brigades were established to visit patients at home and collect samples for testing, and 25 emergency centers were contracted to visit and transport patients with COVID-19 symptoms. Overall, in 2020, the group of providers contracted for COVID-19 packages covered 507 hospitals and 950 mobile brigades.[25] In addition, the NHSU introduced a separate package to provide hospitals with transitional financial support. These transitional payments consisted of two parts. One was available to hospitals whose historical budgets had shrunk in 2020 as a result of the COVID-19–related loss of service utilization and the transition to

NHSU rates. Such losses were fully covered July through September 2020 and covered by at least 90 percent in the following months. The second part of the transitional support package was available to all NHSU contractors in specialized care to compensate for the extra workload on medical personnel resulting from the pandemic. These payments were defined based on the actual staff numbers of the facilities, assuming an across-the-board increase in their salaries.

Providers are expected to provide free medications for inpatient services covered in the PMG using their own budgets and medicines provided free by the MoH through centralized procurement, but in practice, a large share of medications is funded out-of-pocket (OOP). All specialized care packages except outpatient care are specified to explicitly cover medications. Providers are therefore expected to pay for the necessary medicines out of their budgets. On top of hospital-level procurement, they can also use medicines and medical goods procured centrally by the MoH and provided free to facilities through the centralized procurement program, which is separate from the PMG and implemented by the MoH through the state-owned enterprise, "Medical Procurement of Ukraine."[26] Historically, a significant share of medications used during specialized care was paid by the patients OOP (see "The Role of Private, Out-of-Pocket Spending" in chapter 2). No statistics are yet available to determine whether this practice changed in 2020 with the PMG rollout of specialized care. The NHSU has widely and publicly communicated that priority acute inpatient services, including medicines, were protected from any form of co-payment but has remained less specific about the expectation regarding other services in the PMG.

Payment for specialized care through the PMG

Hospitals contracted for the specialized care packages are required to be legally autonomous from the state to create a purchaser-provider split and remove conflicts of interest, but this has also highlighted the need to strengthen facility governance and accountability. The reform of specialized care payments is the first time that specialized care is being purchased from providers that are legally autonomous from the state. This includes communal not-for-profit enterprises or private entities. The requirement was a critical component of the reform agenda, removing the conflict of interest from service purchasing and increasing financial and managerial flexibility in the delivery of services. The first year of implementation of this new arrangement has highlighted the need to strengthen facility governance at the local level to increase transparency and accountability. For example, their autonomous legal status has allowed communal hospitals to keep their budgets in commercial banks rather than in the treasury. Many hospitals have used this arrangement to develop substantial bank deposits instead of increasing current spending on salaries or investment, for example. Without strong accountability mechanisms at the local level, it remains unclear whether such decisions were in the best interest of patients. This current weakness in accountability means that there may also be other distortions in the use of resources at the provider level that jeopardize efficiency. Regulations on autonomous provider status require further refinement to ensure that hospitals are held duly accountable.

For the 2020 contracts, the NHSU stipulated a range of service delivery requirements for providers wanting to deliver each of the 29 specialized care packages. There are a number of universal requirements—for example, related to legal status, licensing, and e-Health functionalities—and package-specific requirements related to the characteristics of the facility, medical personnel, availability of relevant equipment, and additional relevant licenses, such as for nuclear energy or the use of narcotics. Given the absence of an integrated service delivery model, contract specifications in 2020 drew on policies available in various existing strategic documents. For example, the EMC package incorporated some of the principles in the "Concept for EMC Development,"[27] such as limiting EMC to life-threatening conditions, development of phone counseling, and coordination with PHC and other relevant specialists such as mental health professionals to refer cases to where emergency response is not required. However, neither the contract specifications nor the respective payment mechanisms contained provisions to guide and incentivize referral or integrated care delivery. In 2020, contracts were signed with a majority of existing communal providers, specifically 1,631 specialized care providers, including 55 private facilities and 25 oblast-level EMC centers.[28] Contracts are valid for a year, and facilities apply for new contracts for each service on an annual basis, except for contracts that were introduced in 2020 in response to the COVID-19 pandemic or to provide financial support to hospitals experiencing losses.

From April 2020, most of the specialized care in PMG-2020 (80.8 percent) was purchased using global budgets.[29] Previously, SNGs paid for specialized care at hospitals using line-item budgeting. From April 2020, the NHSU used global budgets to pay for 67.1 percent of the entire number of payments made to fund the PMG or 80.8 percent of spending on specialized care, as illustrated in figure 3.8. This included EMC, COVID-related care, and all other services except diagnostic procedures and inpatient care. For each PMG package contracted on a global budget, the NHSU defined a "base rate" per one service unit—for example, per one case treated in a hospital, one outpatient service, or one resident of an area covered by an EMC center. This base rate was multiplied by the number of services the contractor provided in the previous year according to formally reported statistics. The base rates were sometimes adjusted to account for the variation of costs across service types. For example, the outpatient base rate was

FIGURE 3.8

Payment mix for PMG services in Q2–Q3 of 2020

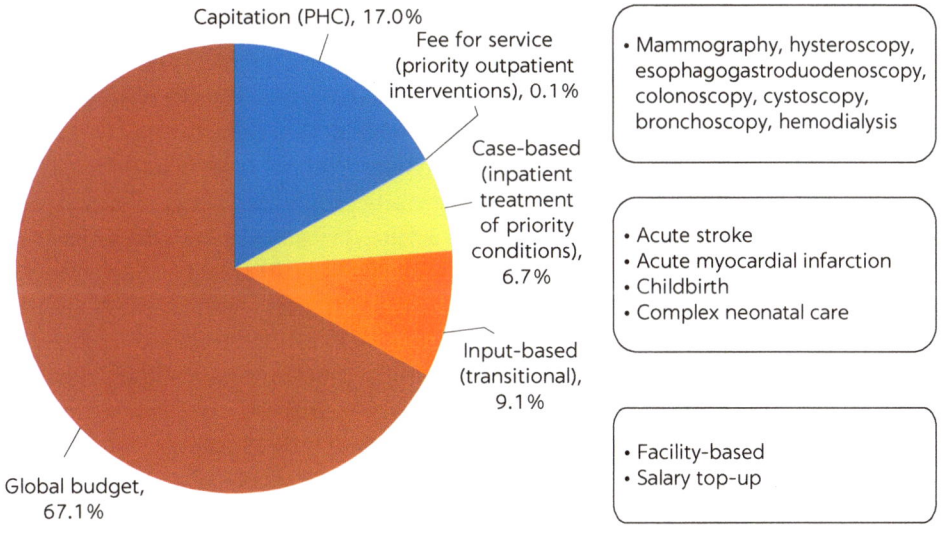

Source: NHSU dashboard, "Payments to medical service providers," part 6, https://nszu.gov.ua/e-data/dashboard /pmg-pay.

multiplied by 9.713 if the service included a surgical procedure and by 0.186 if it was a dental care intervention. For each service for which they were contracted, the provider received a budget equivalent to the base rate times the number of services multiplied by any adjustment factors.

Defining base rates has been a technical challenge given the lack of reliable data, including cost information. The base rates used in global budget calculations were defined through a combination of historical budgets and specific costing studies. In 2018, a top-down costing approach was applied in 180 (volunteer) hospitals representing approximately 90 percent of the total in three oblasts—Poltava, Odesa, and Lviv. Another study estimated underfinancing of inpatient medicines using a bottom-up approach. These results were used to set payment rates for the 131 groups that were the starting point in the transition based on Australian Refined DRGs (NHSU 2020). At least some of the rates were also influenced by additional costing analysis to incorporate more advanced treatment protocols, as was the case for the TB treatment package. The work on package pricing was further complicated by the lack of reliable data on service utilization and facility-level financing.

The decision to use base rates to define payment levels in 2020 led to palpable changes in the planned amounts of funding the hospitals had traditionally received, which was meant to incentivize hospital optimization and efficiency gains. The NHSU chose a relatively temperate approach, spreading the funds thinly across about four-fifths of all facilities and almost cutting out the rest. It anticipated that 43 percent of the hospitals currently dealing with 60 percent of hospitalizations would receive an increase. Another 16 percent to 24 percent of all hospitalizations were expected to retain 70 percent to 90 percent of their historical budgets, thereby experiencing moderate cuts. At the same time, 13 percent of the hospitals would get only 50 percent to 70 percent of the historical budgets and would have to reorganize. The largest cuts would be borne by 382 mono-profile facilities—large hospitals focused on treating a single condition, such as TB or HIV/AIDS, and together accounting for 21 percent of all hospitals whose operations needed to go through major transformations.

The NHSU had initially intended to gradually introduce elements of DRG-based payments for hospitals in May 2020, but this plan was postponed and eventually canceled for 2020, due to the focus on tackling the COVID-19 pandemic. Therefore, in 2020, the NHSU used exclusively global budgets as the payment method for nonpriority hospital care. The original PMG-2020 design assumed that during this first year the NHSU would gradually introduce UDRG-based payments.[30] Starting from May 2020, the payment was to be split into a global budget and a case-based amount, with the share of the latter gradually expanding from 10 percent to 40 percent by July 2020. In parallel, providers were requested to start coding and reporting their cases by the UDRG. However, in June the government postponed introducing the DRG into facility payments until October, and in September it decided to cancel it entirely for 2020. Two reasons were given. First, the UDRG grouping of 131 categories was evaluated as excessively broad, leaving a high degree of cost-heterogeneity within individual groups. Second, hospital-level financial risks from transitioning to case-rate payments would have been exacerbated by the COVID-19 pandemic, which was expected to depress the utilization of essential services. Hospitals were still required to report cases by DRGs. The NHSU's automated verification system showed that, as of September 2020, only 0.73 percent of the reported cases were marked as visibly erroneous and returned to hospitals, but further analysis of the quality and completeness of these reports is required via manual review, which has not yet been conducted.

Inpatient treatment of priority conditions was funded based on case rates and, reportedly, priced to cover a wider range of costs. In addition to global budgets, the four priority conditions—acute stroke, acute myocardial infarction, childbirth, and complex neonatal care—require inpatient treatment for which hospitals receive case-based payments. Reportedly, the NHSU defined the case rates for these priority conditions based on complementary studies using a bottom-up costing method to ensure that the rates cover full costs of required essential medicines and medical products as well as diagnostic tests. Altogether, contracts for treatment of these four conditions accounted for 6.7 percent of the entire contracted budget in PMG-2020, equivalent to 8.1 percent of all specialized care contracts.

The NHSU also paid fee-for-service for seven outpatient services in order to incentivize provision. Outpatient endoscopies, mammography, and hemodialysis were also paid through fee-for-service. This approach was chosen deliberately to stimulate the supply of diagnostic endoscopies and mammography services and to promote early detection and treatment of NCDs by incentivizing providers to invest in required equipment. Overall, contracts for services paid via fee-for-service accounted for only 0.1 percent of all PMG-2020 contract volume and 0.1 percent of specialized care.

The global budget was also used for COVID-19 packages because of the lack of predictability of case numbers. In 2021, the planned value of contracts for COVID-19 care (excluding COVID-19 vaccination) was UAH 16.6 billion (13 percent of the total PMG budget). COVID-19 vaccination services were paid on fee-for-service basis for each episode of COVID-19 vaccine administration to patients; the total planned value of the COVID-19 vaccination package in 2021 was about UAH 1.5 billion.

Finally, as discussed earlier, in 2020, the government provided hospitals with two forms of additional financial support to offset losses associated with the health financing reform and COVID-19. The decision to grant support to loss-making hospitals was made on the grounds that the coinciding impact of the health financing reforms and the COVID-19 outbreak may have exposed hospitals to a greater degree of financial vulnerability than would have been the case if the reforms had been implemented before the pandemic. Specifically, it led to the drying up of two of the important sources of financing that hospitals previously received, namely, local budgets and patients. Not all local governments have transferred the allocated resources from their local budgets to hospitals, and some have reduced historical co-financing. Also, many hospitals suspended planned health procedures and interventions for the duration of the pandemic, and patients have also, likely of their own choice, forgone care that is not necessary, reducing hospital and provider revenues both formal and informal. The additional government funding covered:

- Lump-sum top-ups to avoid catastrophic losses due to hospital payment reform. The first amendment, in June 2020 (effective in July), was aimed to ensure that providers do not bear substantial losses as a result of the reform, raising their budgets to at least 90 percent of the amount they have historically received through the central government grant. This type of support was granted to 519 communal facilities and amounted to 1.6 percent of the PMG-2020 contract volume (UAH 2.1 billion).

- Top-ups to fund salary increases during COVID-19. In June 2020, CabMin issued a resolution introducing mandatory salary top-ups for health care workers in specialized care for the period of September–December 2020, compensating for the additional workload and risk resulting from the COVID-19 pandemic.[31] To fund these top-ups, the PMG package for transitional financial support was extended to include an additional component to cover the top-ups. The value of the top-ups was calculated based on the actual personnel numbers in each hospital and amounted to salary increases of 70 percent for doctors, 50 percent for nurses, and 30 percent for junior medical staff. To become eligible for these additional funds, facilities were required to demonstrate that they had prepared a strategic development plan approved by the facility owner.

Both types of transitional financial support to providers were extended for the first quarter of 2021 but entirely discontinued starting from April 2021.

Recommendations

Short term

- Unbundle the broadly defined packages for outpatient, inpatient surgical, inpatient nonsurgical, and emergency care packages into more explicitly defined packages of care. For the remaining services in these four packages, specifications need to be enhanced to spell out what conditions are covered in such packages.
- Consider regrouping packages that represent inputs into other services into comprehensive packages to treat specific conditions. For example, instead of the current packages for chemotherapy and radiotherapy services, it may be more effective to develop a specification of a whole pathway for diagnosis and treatment of different cancers.
- In addition, unbundle some of the existing DRGs. Many of them are neither clinically similar nor cost-homogeneous, leading to significant cost variation across cases and possible financial risk. Investments in coding and the fullness of information collected with the use of DRG classifications are key for further refinement of DRG-based payments.
- Continue to strengthen the NHSU's monitoring and evaluation systems to routinely undertake data quality checks, spot abnormalities in service utilization patterns, and do trend monitoring to identify miscoding, upcoding, and abuse by providers or patients.
- To transition to greater reliance on DRG payments, develop a clear transition pathway that provides facilities with protection against excessive financial risk and gives them time to adjust as needed, including developing their coding capacities and adjusting their clinical practice. Ad hoc financing top-ups should be avoided, especially when they are in the form of input-based support to providers, such as the salary top-ups introduced to manage the COVID-19 shock from September 2020 through March 2021. Options include using risk corridors, paying partly by DRGs and partly by global budgets, and providing feedback to hospitals on their performance, how service delivery can be adjusted for greater efficiency, and how to deal with unexpected threats such as the COVID-19 pandemic.
- Strengthen governance and accountability regulations for providers to balance their autonomous status and prevent the use of financing received

within PMG for inappropriate objectives, like long-term deposits of funds, instead of increasing salaries or investing in service delivery improvements.

Medium term

- Develop, approve, and implement an integrated service delivery strategy for specialized care, coordinating it with PHC and public health. Such a strategy would need to consist of a broad concept endorsed at the cabinet level to ensure that the proposed approach is fiscally sustainable; is linked with reforms in other sectors such as primary social care and education; and includes a realistic model for joined-up service planning, funding, and delivery with SNGs. The strategy would lead to legislative changes to facilitate an introduction of the new practices and structures and enforce the duty of the involved parties to cooperate.
- Review the existing Capable Network Plan to ensure a more transparent selection methodology and to ensure that inclusion criteria are aligned with the policy principles for the network's development, such as ensuring sufficient service volumes, avoiding fragmentation, and equity of geographic access. The ultimate pathway for the changes in the hospital network should be the coordinated outcome of MoH-led policy imperatives, regional planning by subnational stakeholders, and strategic purchasing by the NHSU.
- Review selective contracting of providers, in which providers get to choose which packages they want to deliver. This potentially skews service provision toward more profitable services, creating asymmetries in supply and demand and problems in service availability. Instead, region-level need assessments should guide decisions about qualities and types of care needed and serve as a basis for contracting by the NHSU. Patient entitlement and guarantee of services to patients are critical. Providers in the Capable Network Plan should be required to provide all services appropriate to their level. Complementing this with multiyear contracts, rather than the current annual contracts, would also give providers the incentive to invest in the inputs needed to provide services more efficiently.

NOTES

1. The national health information system was launched under the Cabinet of Ministers Order No. 411 of April 25, 2018. Access the full text at https://zakon.rada.gov.ua/laws/show/411-2018-%D0%BF.
2. Cabinet of Ministers of Ukraine. Про затвердження переліку платних послуг, які надаються в державних і комунальних закладах охорони здоров'я та вищих медичних навчальних закладах [On approval of the list of paid services which is provided in the state and municipal health care facilities and higher medical educational institutions] (in Ukrainian). Resolution No. 1138; September 17, 1996. Kyiv: Verkhovna Rada of Ukraine, 1996, located at https://zakon.rada.gov.ua/laws/show/1138-96-%D0%BF#Text. Accessed June 4, 2021
3. Registration of people with PHC physicians/providers (population enrolment rules) is regulated by MoH Order 503 of 2018.
4. Data are from the NHSU open data, available at https://edata.e-health.gov.ua/e-data/dashboard (in Ukrainian).
5. Data are from the NHSU open data, available at https://edata.e-health.gov.ua/e-data/dashboard (in Ukrainian).

6. There are no public solo practices in Ukraine. There are two types of PHC providers. Each of the first type is an umbrella entity; most are public, and a few are private. The second type is all private solo practices.

7. PHC delivery is regulated by MoH Orders 503 and 504 of 2018, located at https://zakon .rada.gov.ua/laws/show/z0347-18#Tex and https://zakon.rada.gov.ua/laws/show /z0348-18#Text respectively.

8. Telemedicine at the PHC level is broadly conceptualized as a combination of digital administrative tools (such as E-Health) plus digital tools for consultations and /communicating primary diagnostic data.

9. The text of this law may be accessed at https://zakon.rada.gov.ua/laws/show /2206-19#Text.

10. From 110–120%, the capitation rate declines to 0.8; from 120–130%, to 0.6; from 130–140%, to 0.4; from 140–150%, to 0.2; and then 0 if it exceeds 150%.

11. Data are from the NHSU dashboard, accessed at https://edata.e-health.gov.ua/e-data /dashboard.

12. For the complete list, see MoH Order No. 504 of 19.03.2018, "On approving the rules for provision of primary health care," located at https://zakon.rada.gov.ua/laws/show /z0348-18#Text.

13. The list of medicines covered by AMP and the procedures for prescription, provision, and reimbursement of these medicines are regulated by CMU Resolution No. 152 of 17.03.2017, located at https://zakon.rada.gov.ua/laws/show/152-2017-%D0%BF#Text.

14. The guidelines were provided in the Cabinet of Ministers Resolution No. 1300 of December 23, 2020, located at https://zakon.rada.gov.ua/laws/show/1300-2020-%D0%BF#Text.

15. The methodology and procedures are described in an NHSU order of January 28, 2020.

16. More precisely, the transitional measures were intended to cap losses at zero during July and August 2020, and at a minimum of 10 percent October through December 2020. During this time, the NHSU would cover 90–100 percent of the losses, depending on the rate at which the facility was implementing its agreed-on transformation plan.

17. Data are taken from the MoH Centre for Medical Statistics (http://medstat.gov.ua/ukr /main.html) and OECD Statistics (https://stats.oecd.org/).

18. Data are taken from the MoH Centre for Medical Statistics (http://medstat.gov.ua/ukr /main.html) and OECD Statistics (https://stats.oecd.org/).

19. Data are taken from the MoH Centre for Medical Statistics (http://medstat.gov.ua/ukr /main.html) and OECD Statistics (https://stats.oecd.org/).

20. Data are taken from the MoH Centre for Medical Statistics (http://medstat.gov.ua/ukr /main.html).

21. Data are taken from the MoH Centre for Medical Statistics (http://medstat.gov.ua/ukr /main.html).

22. Data are taken from the MoH Centre for Medical Statistics (http://medstat.gov.ua/ukr /main.html).

23. Data are taken from the State Statistics Service of Ukraine.

24. Data are taken from the MoH Centre for Medical Statistics (http://medstat.gov.ua/ukr /main.html).

25. Data were derived from the NHSU dashboard, located at https://nszu.gov.ua/e-data /dashboard/pmg-pay.

26. Centralized procurement of medicines and medical goods is a program under the MoH (Code: 2301400), implemented by a state-owned enterprise, Medical Procurement of Ukraine. The state-owned enterprise procures medicines and medical goods based on the list approved by the MoH based on requests by medical facilities. More information on this process can be found in CabMin Resolution No. 298 of 17.03.2011, https://zakon.rada.gov .ua/laws/show/298-2011-%D0%BF#Text.

27. Complete text can be found at https://zakon.rada.gov.ua/laws/show /383-2019-%D1%80#Text.

28. Data are from the NHSU open data dashboard, https://edata.e-health.gov.ua/e-data /dashboard.

29. Here and further in this report, figures describing the composition of payment methods in the PMG refer to NHSU payments during the second and third quarters of 2020.

30. The list of UDRGs is approved by the CabMin, and it is part of the procedure of implementing the PMG. DRGs are constructed using Australian Refined DRGs (V.9.0 and the list of relevant classifications [diagnoses and surgical interventions]) is customized for

Ukraine. The NHSU is responsible for fine-tuning and developing the UDRG grouping algorithm. Each clinical group / UDRG is assigned a payment rate and cost-weight.

31. The resolution was issued by the Cabinet of Ministers through Resolution #610 of 19.06.2020. Full text is available at https://zakon.rada.gov.ua/laws/show /610-2020-%D0%BF#Text.

REFERENCES

Ministry of Health of Ukraine. 2019. Як застосовувати телемедицину лікарям первинної ланки: методичні рекомендації [How primary care physicians should apply telemedicine: guidelines]. August 22. https://moz.gov.ua/article/for-medical-staff/jak-zastosovuvati-telemedicinu -likarjam-pervinnoi-lanki-metodichni-rekomendacii.

Ministry of Health of Ukraine. n.d. "Concept of Primary Health Care Development in Ukraine to 2031." Unpublished manuscript.

NHSU (National Health Service of Ukraine). 2020. *NHSU Guidebook: PMG Packages—Approach to Contracting Medical Facilities*. February 7. https://nszu.gov.ua/storage/editor/files /paketi-medichnikh-poslug-07022020_1581100466.pdf.

WHO (World Health Organization) and Ministry of Health of Ukraine. 2020. "White Paper on Health Service Delivery in Ukraine." Unpublished manuscript.

4 Governance of the Program of Medical Guarantees

The creation of a health service–purchasing agency, such as the National Health Service of Ukraine (NHSU), along with the introduction into the health system of the strategic purchasing function, necessitates changes in governance structures. The key functions of these governance structures should be to set the strategic direction for the purchasing agency and to hold it accountable for resource use and results.

Five aspects of governance are essential to enable this. These are:

- Autonomy of the purchasing agency with respect to technical and operational matters, subject to government authority on policy and setting strategic objectives.
- Clarity and transparency in roles for government bodies involved in policy and oversight of the NHSU—notably, the Cabinet of Ministries (CabMin), the Ministry of Health (MoH), and the Ministry of Finance (MoF)—together with explicit, transparent methodologies, rules, and processes for decision-making.
- External accountability and effective oversight, with clear lines of accountability and citizen participation.
- Effective systems of internal control and risk management within a firm and credible budget constraints.
- Well-coordinated and constructive interagency relationships between the purchaser and the ministries responsible for health and finance policies as well as with the subnational (local) governments (SNGs) responsible for health facilities, which in Ukraine are also involved in co-financing health care.

In addition, adequate capacity of all agencies involved in governance arrangements in terms of personnel and other resources is a prerequisite not only for effective performance but also to underpin meaningful reporting on performance, review, and evaluation. Strengthening the quality and availability of NHSU data, as well as its capacity for data analysis, is another important aspect that will provide information of value to the MoH in exercising its stewardship over the sector and ensuring good governance of providers.

This chapter will examine each of these five features of good governance as they pertain to the NHSU as the purchasing agent of the Program of Medical Guarantees (PMG), as well as issues of institutional capacity.

THE AUTONOMY OF THE NHSU

The MoH undertook a rigorous evaluation of alternatives before deciding to establish the NHSU as a central executive agency (CEA). The process took into consideration both Ukrainian law and experience as well as international practices. The options considered were a department within the central office of the MoH; a CEA, a state nonprofit enterprise; and an off-budget trust fund, a nonprofit self-governing organization (Maynzyuk and Dzhygyr 2016). In 2017, the NHSU was established as a CEA under Law 2168.

As a purchaser of health care services, the option of a CEA was considered the most appropriate for a number of reasons. First, as a separate agency from the MoH and SNGs, the NHSU would be more likely to act solely in the best interests of patients, avoiding the conflicts of interest that could arise if the purchaser owned health care providers or had responsibilities for health facility staff, as the MoH and SNGs do. Second, a CEA would be directly accountable to the government. In effect, CabMin would regulate NHSU activities to ensure that it operated under unified, transparent, and fair rules of purchasing and payment and managed budget funds based on maximum transparency, accountability, and its budget obligations (supported by the treasury) in accordance with requirements approved by CabMin. Third, as a supervisory tax-financed purchaser, the NHSU did not need to have a supervisory board with employer and employee representatives, which is recommended if the purchaser is funded by payroll contributions. Although there are examples of supervisory boards with other representation, this would have required a different and more autonomous legal status in Ukraine law, which might be considered in the future after the NHSU has developed management capacity and a track record. However, as discussed later in this chapter, it would be beneficial to strengthen the role of the citizen and taxpayer and to have patient representatives participate in formal NHSU oversight and accountability. Fourth, once political approval of the scope of the benefit package and its tariffs had been given, the purchaser would have the managerial autonomy to purchase health services decisions within that framework, based on technical criteria of medical grounds, standards, and rules of payment, as well as be protected from political influence at the central and subnational levels. Fifth, compared to state enterprises or off-budget trust funds, there is greater government control over the budget and financial management of a CEA, which reduces fiscal risks.

As laid out in Law 2168, the NHSU has autonomy for technical and operational matters, balanced with accountability ex post for performance and use of resources, while the government retains authority over policy decisions and fiscal resources for the NHSU. The intention of the law was for the NHSU to provide politically neutral, objective technical analysis and advice to government authorities on policy matters, and then after receiving this information, the government would make decisions. The NHSU should faithfully implement policy and manage within the resources allocated to it by the state budget.

Regulations adopted subsequent to Law 2168, especially during 2019, helped to make progress in clarifying the NHSU's autonomy.

The creation of the NHSU also means that changes are needed in the roles of other agencies of the government, especially the MoH and MoF. The MoH, for example, needs to transition to a role that is primarily about approving health financing policies as part of its health sector stewardship function and its governance task of setting health financing strategy. In this way, it can give direction to the NHSU and participate in the oversight of the NHSU's performance. The transition for the MoH and MoF to these more "arm's-length" stewardship and governance roles is not yet complete. During the transition, there is a risk that the MoH will continue to work under old business processes and intervene inappropriately in the operational and technical matters of the NHSU. Equally, the NHSU needs to respect the boundaries between their technical advisory role and the political authority over policy and strategy assigned to the MoH. The transition has been challenging, and these new relationships and governance arrangements have not yet stabilized.

It can take some time for the different entities of government to achieve a shared and stable understanding of the extent of the NHSU's autonomy and the boundary between policy and implementation. Still, as discussions during subsequent government transitions have shown, this understanding is not yet widely shared. As in many other countries that have recently established social health insurance or purchasing agencies, the MoH finds it difficult to develop a clear understanding of how it can steer health policy and strategy when most of the health budget is channeled through a separate purchasing agency and most service delivery is managed by local authorities. Chapter 2 recommended the development of a long-term health financing strategy. Such a strategy is vital for good governance, too. The current lack of a health sector strategy and a health financing strategy, in particular, makes it difficult for the MoH to set direction as part of its new governance responsibility for the NHSU.

In most countries, it normally takes some time for these new roles and processes to become mature and stable across changes of government and ministry leadership. This maturation and stability can be supported by frequent and effective policy briefing and dialogue processes for new MoH and MoF leadership by building professional staff capacity for their new stewardship and governance roles and by building broad-based constituencies of support for the health financing strategy.

CLEAR AND TRANSPARENT ROLES, METHODOLOGIES, AND PROCESSES FOR DECISION-MAKING

As chapter 2 explained, a key task of these methodologies and processes is to arrive at a PMG and an associated budget allocation to the NHSU that are consistent with each other, leading to a credible fiscal constraint as well as an efficient allocation of resources for health care. This will help ensure that communication about the PMG to citizens does not raise unrealistic expectations about the range of services and level of out-of-pocket expenses they can expect.

The respective roles of the CabMin, MoH, MoF, and NHSU in decision-making related to the PMG were set out in Law 2168. These roles include decision-making with respect to the NHSU budget, the PMG benefit package, payment methods, tariffs, and contracting providers. The law includes important checks and balances. As in most countries, details on the methodologies and processes for decision-making are set out in regulations, rather than in the law itself.

In 2019, important progress was made in clarifying rules and processes, but gaps remain. Orders of the CabMin clarified rules concerning contracting of providers, including developing contract specifications, tariff-setting, and rules for sharing medical records and data between the NHSU, MoH, and providers. The NHSU has subsequently developed associated business processes. One persistent gap is the lack of any systematic methodology for defining PMG priorities, developing the benefit package, and establishing the contract specifications for various services contracted by the NHSU. These contract specifications are the NHSU's main tool for strategic purchasing to drive efficiency, modernization, and quality improvement. The processes for developing the PMG and contract specifications need to be systematic and evidence-informed. The processes also need to look at costs, benefits, and affordability within the NHSU's budget constraints.

In addition, to enhance the transparency and legitimacy of the development of the PMG and contract specifications, a clear framework needs to be put in place to govern the processes of consultation with medical experts and patient representatives and how their input feeds into formal decision-making on the PMG. The MoH and NHSU need to strengthen mechanisms for consultations with stakeholders and to find ways to include patient representatives before decisions are made on the benefit package and contract specifications. While consultations take place during the service package discussions, these mostly consist of experts and providers. Patients are represented in the recently established Public Control Council (PCC) (discussed further below), which reviews and discusses the PMG overall and individual service packages, including payment methods and rates. However, the consultation process needs to be further developed to avoid the risk of generating recommendations for health care that are unaffordable, inefficient, or of insufficient quality. Conflicts of interest and undue influence of special interests can occur if consultation processes are dominated by particular interest groups and if the consultations are not managed within a clear framework that prioritizes evidence on efficient, cost-effective, and equitable care. Unless this process is disciplined by a clear framework for decision-making, there is likely to be a tendency to expand the number and range of services and of hospitals and other facilities that can provide contracted services. This will spread health budget resources too thinly across an extensive network of facilities, and the efficiency gains that strategic purchasing can achieve will fail to be realized.

There also needs to be a medium-term process for planning, priority setting, and budgeting regarding the PMG that goes beyond the current annual process provided by Law 2168, which is linked to the annual state budget process. A medium-term vision for the development of the PMG, tariffs, and the Affordable Medicines Program (AMP) is needed to schedule time for analysis, consultation, and implementation in coordination with the budget cycle. The NHSU's prioritization and budget formulation will also need to reflect improved methodologies and approaches for the PMG benefit package development and contract specification recommended above.

EXTERNAL ACCOUNTABILITY AND OVERSIGHT OF THE NHSU

As an autonomous CEA, the NHSU is subordinate and accountable to the CabMin. The law establishing the NHSU gives the MoH and MoF joint authority over key policy decisions governing health financing and NHSU purchasing, including approval of the PMG, tariff, and budget proposals. At the same time, the NHSU is a spending unit secondary to the MoH and as such submits all policy and expenditure proposals and reports to the MoF and the CabMin through the MoH. But the absence of a forum in which the MoH and MoF come together to reach a coherent consensus on health financing strategy and policy before proposals are put to the CabMin impedes the development of a shared strategic vision for health financing. Therefore, an earlier section of this report proposed the creation of an NHSU oversight committee, composed of MoH and MoF representatives and ideally also a representative of the Prime Minister's Office—for example, the deputy prime minister for regions, who has related responsibilities—to address this.

In addition, the NHSU reports to the PCC, whose membership represents patients and civil society. Law 2168 stipulates that PCC membership should be selected by open, transparent competition, and there are provisions to avoid a conflict of interest of council members. Among the PCC's responsibilities are monitoring of activities and performance of the NHSU, reviewing reports prepared by the NHSU, and producing and publishing written findings and recommendations. It thus plays an important role in promoting transparency, which helps reinforce that the NHSU's ultimate accountability is to citizens, as taxpayers and patients. However, the PCC's role is only an advisory one; it does not have the governance powers or responsibilities of a supervisory board. The PCC's role in accountability could be strengthened by linking the PCC to formal oversight by the MoH and CabMin and better defining its role. A CabMin order that sets out the details of the PCC's role, the reports that the NHSU should share with the PCC, and the findings and reports that the PCC should provide to the government could be considered. This order could also establish a formal mechanism by which the PCC can report to the MoH and CabMin, such as via the proposed oversight committee mentioned earlier. The CabMin committee overseeing the NHSU, if established, could periodically meet with the PCC chair and members.

For the NHSU to be held accountable, ideally it also needs to have a set of annual and medium-term performance objectives that are aligned with the government's health systems' goals and are realistic given the NHSU's resources. Reporting by the NHSU currently focuses mainly on the budget and approval of the PMG plus other matters on an ad hoc basis. This means there is no integrated, coherent regular mechanism of ex post accountability by which the NHSU reports to the CabMin on all aspects of performance. Ukraine is currently introducing a new system of performance-based oversight of policy implementation by the CabMin that will strengthen the accountability of the ministries for executing sector strategies. This would create more transparent objectives for the NHSU, integrated within health sector policy, and a framework to report against these objectives through the MoH. Given the early stage of the development of this performance-based system, it would be helpful to pilot the precise mechanism, including relevant aspects of sector policy implementation to be measured and responsibilities for agreeing on and tracking progress on performance objectives and indicators. These objectives need to recognize the reality that there will be a transition period before the full vision for the PMG is realized. Accordingly, performance monitoring for the NHSU should focus on whether the NHSU is allocating its resources in a way that best achieves improvement and progress toward its statutory objectives for population health, access to health care, and equity.

An external audit of the NHSU by the State Audit Authority, National Anti-Corruption Committee, and the Accounting Chamber of Ukraine is being implemented as mandated, and the NHSU is responsive to its recommendations. While reports of the Accounting Chamber and Anti-Corruption Committee are published, the other audit documents are internal to the government. Good practice would be to also make all audit results publicly available and to publish the NHSU's responses to them.

EFFECTIVE SYSTEMS OF INTERNAL CONTROL WITHIN A FIRM AND CREDIBLE BUDGET CONSTRAINT

For the NHSU to achieve as much as possible with the resources available to it and also be accountable for its performance, it is vital that there be clear internal controls and discipline that prevent breaches of the budget constraint and inappropriate use of resources by the NHSU and the facilities that it contracts. In addition, the NHSU's budget must be credible. This requires the NHSU to use appropriate data and methods in forecasting demand; costing the PMG; and formulating its budget proposal; and the government (on the advice of the MoF and the MoH) ensures that the approved budget is realistic relative to the costs of the PMG.

The NHSU developed and continues to strengthen internal control procedures and measures to prevent mistakes and fraud in claims. The internal controls that the NHSU has put in place include:

- Independent checks and balances, some of which are subject to approval by the MoH and the MoF, within the business processes for each of the stages of purchasing—contracting, payment, and accounting. All internal business processes are documented.
- An internal audit unit that reports to the CEO and is responsible for reviewing and providing assurance of internal control systems and for investigating possible fraud and corruption, although the judicial authorities have responsibility for investigation and prosecution of criminal cases.
- An anti-fraud program (managed by the internal audit unit) that uses automated monitoring based on algorithms to detect potentially fraudulent claims. For example, it generates indicators of overprescribing, fraudulent prescription claims, and inflation of the number of primary care patients. There are also indicators of fraud and inappropriate utilization in common specialized inpatient conditions, such as stroke, myocardial infarction, therapeutic oncology, and complex neonatal care; the development of algorithms for other areas of specialized care is ongoing.

Automated monitoring is supposed to be followed up by monitoring visits to investigate cases, and the frequency of these should be increased. This will, in turn, require strengthening the NHSU's five subnational offices as well as the adoption and implementation of draft by-laws (already prepared) to create the basis for imposing sanctions and penalties on providers.

It would also be good practice for the NHSU executive to develop a risk register to document strategic, financial, operational, and reputational risks and the corresponding risk management measures that would be reviewed regularly by the internal audit unit.

WELL-COORDINATED AND CONSTRUCTIVE INTERAGENCY RELATIONSHIPS

Well-coordinated, constructive interagency relationships—particularly with the MoH, the MoF, and the CabMin—are a key success factor for good governance and high performance in strategic health purchasing. Coordination and constructive relationships at the national level are important to ensure the government sets a coherent strategy and policy for the NHSU. This is not only a matter of good processes for meetings and communications but also about having a shared strategic plan and agreed-upon policy frameworks to guide the respective contributions of the MoH, NHSU, health care providers, and SNGs. The Ukrainian health sector lacks a strategic plan, developed and agreed to by the MoH, the NHSU, and key health sector stakeholders, and endorsed by the government. There is a need to coordinate the activities of the MoF, the MoH, the CabMin, and the NHSU when it comes to setting and agreeing on the health financing strategy and aligning it with wider health sector strategic plans, the NHSU's own institutional plans, new policies, budgets, and frameworks for reporting and accountability.

Building constructive relationships and well-coordinated working arrangements as early as possible after transitions of government or minister is important for several aspects of good governance discussed above. Transitions often present challenges to the stability of policy and strategy as well as leadership. Conflict or lack of alignment between the NHSU and MoH can have the effect of pushing more responsibility for health sector stewardship onto the MoF, which is responsible for ensuring an affordable fiscal constraint and for encouraging efficient use of budget resources. Constructive relationships between the MoH and MoF help strengthen the strategic stewardship role and NHSU governance.

Relationships with SNGs are also important because there remains a significant share of financing that flows through SNGs for health care providers of PMG services and because SNGs are responsible for developing and maintaining their network of health facilities to meet the contractual requirements of the NHSU. Contrary to the original policy intent, the budget code is now worded in ways that create an overlap between the NHSU and SNG expenditure assignment. While the ability of SNGs to provide supplementary finance to fill gaps and address local bottlenecks and service needs has been a useful coping mechanism during the COVID crisis, this creates a suboptimal set of incentives for the longer term. It has adverse implications for accountability.

As owners of facilities, SNGs are responsible for the deficits and debts of their health facilities. The NHSU, SNG representatives, and the MoF recognize the need for a transition period for providers to eliminate their deficits through efficiency improvements and staff reassignment or transfer; they also recognize that there is a need for coordination between the NHSU and SNGs on this.

Over the medium to long term, even better coordination of SNGs and hospital districts with the NHSU will be needed as oblasts implement more substantial measures to rationalize the facility network. This coordination could involve the NHSU's five subnational branch offices, each of which covers three to eight oblasts[1] working with and through hospital districts. This is a very large and long-term agenda for change. It may therefore be appropriate to begin with one or a few demonstration sites in oblasts where there is already some political engagement with and technical support for master planning and optimization. The detailed architecture of the new hospital districts is still being designed.

There are many challenges to be addressed in the governance of newly autonomous health care facilities. The development of external accountability mechanisms and internal control for health care facilities is a vital complementary reform to NHSU governance so that there can be a chain of accountability for improving health system performance, using both contractual accountability via the NHSU and accountability to owners via local governments. The NHSU and local governments have shared interests and can benefit from coordination through data sharing and other initiatives, such as joint facility monitoring visits and coordination of support and sanctions for non-performing health facilities.

NHSU CAPACITY: STRUCTURE, HUMAN RESOURCES, INFORMATION TECHNOLOGY

The NHSU's current level of staffing (266 central and 53 subnational in February 2021) and the size of its administrative budget relative to its program budget for purchasing services (0.23 percent in 2020) are lean by international standards, and it constrains the full development of its strategic purchasing function. Per Decree 85, its aggregate staff ceiling can be expanded to 1,060. The aggregate limit on NHSU staff should be sufficient, although greater flexibility is needed to reallocate posts between its central and five subnational offices (ceilings of 400 and 660 staff members respectively, per decree), in line with NHSU managerial priorities and in response to technological development—for example, greater use of central automation, greater use of online meetings. The practical constraint on staff numbers is due to the NHSU's small administrative budget and difficulty in attracting staff with scarce skills to some of its posts. It is also affected by short-term general limits on public sector hiring. There is no regulation setting an appropriate share of the NHSU budget to be allocated to administration, as found in many countries.

There is also a need for a systematic effort to address the shortages of analytical staff in the NHSU and the MoH, driven in part by the low salary scales relative to the market in segments such as information technology (IT). This is a constraint experienced in all public sector agencies, and it also hampers developing the skills of existing analytical staff. Implementation of plans for the development of NHSU subnational offices is vital for monitoring the performance of providers against contractual requirements and for effective implementation of anti-fraud mechanisms, including checks at the facility level. The NHSU relies on donor support to fill skill gaps by hiring personnel on short-term contracts, as is common in many fiscally constrained lower-middle-income countries. However, it is desirable to build more permanent in-house capacity in these areas and to strengthen the health sector knowledge and experience of existing analysts who can develop the full potential of the NHSU for strategic purchasing over time. The NHSU as an agency can offer somewhat higher salaries than ministry staff for roles that require scarce analytical and IT skills. This is common in many countries and can become a source of tension between agencies unless there is a corresponding effort to address the analytical skill shortages in the MoH and MoF. Human resource policies that allow or even encourage rotation of some staff between the ministries and the purchaser can be helpful. Consideration could be given to strategies such as long-term contracting in/out, temporary reassignment into the NHSU of such skills, rotation of staff between the NHSU and the MoH and MoF, and more attractive remuneration, training opportunities, and career pathways for analysts and IT staff.

Implementation of plans for the NHSU subnational office development is key to monitoring provider performance against contract requirements for counter-fraud mechanisms and strategic purchasing to support service delivery reform. The NHSU has established five subnational offices, as previously described, in line with recommendations in the 2019 review. The heads of these offices have the seniority and profile to represent the NHSU to governors, mayors, hospital directors, and senior government officials. Subnational offices currently have around 5 to 10 staff who have to work with approximately 30 to 50 hospitals in addition to other facilities. The NHSU had planned to increase staffing by 20 to 25 percent in 2021 as the next step to develop their functions and play an expanded role in contract verification, monitoring the fulfillment of contracts, and checking for fraud. For example, subnational office staff are needed to verify that contracted hospitals meet requirements such as license, equipment, and staffing, and then prepare the relevant contract for signature by the central level, which provides an independent check in the process. In the third stage of subnational office development, the NHSU planned that these staff would take responsibility for monitoring fulfillment of contracts, using both electronic document checks and visiting a prioritized list of facilities to check compliance and investigate fraud identified by the central internal audit unit. In the future, as the NHSU further develops strategic purchasing, subnational offices should also play a role in assessing local population health needs, provider capacity to respond to those needs, and the use of contracting power to support reorganization and development of the provider network.

The NHSU faces the challenge of a lack of funding for IT software upgrades and licenses. The agency relies on external funding from development partners for a large share of IT software, while licensing costs for e-Health are a perpetual issue due to the monopoly power of a single developer. The NHSU uses a procurement platform for contracting, and the United States Agency for International Development provided US$3 million for development of the NHSU IT system, which will automate contracting and payment processes. Still, sustainable funding is needed.

In the medium term, as the e-Health system for health care providers is developed further, it will be important to invest in coordinated development of the NHSU's IT and data management systems to interconnect and integrate with the wider e-Health system and avoid duplicative systems. The development of the e-Health system at the health care provider level is still at an early stage.

RECOMMENDATIONS

Short term

- Create a CabMin committee to act as an oversight committee for the NHSU and to facilitate better interagency coordination among the MoF, MoH, NHSU, and other ministries in setting the strategic directions for the NHSU and reaching consensus on issues such as health financing strategy, PMG packages, budget proposals, and tariffs.
- Pilot a mechanism through which the MoH would organize NHSU accountability to the CabMin for relevant aspects of the sector policy implementation, clearly defining responsibilities for agreeing on and reviewing performance objectives. This can form part of Ukraine's new developments in performance-based oversight of policy implementation by the CabMin.
- Develop an NHSU organizational strategy, which should be aligned with the health financing strategy and with the performance objectives and indicators previously proposed in this report by which the NHSU can be held accountable to the CabMin.
- Establish a small, permanent unit in the MoH with technical expertise in health financing policy to enable the MoH to better perform its stewardship and governance roles with respect to the NHSU and its role in the CabMin committee overseeing the NHSU.
- Specify the role and procedures of the PCC with respect to NHSU governance in a CabMin order, including the information and reports the NHSU should share with the PCC; formalize a mechanism by which the PCC can share its findings and recommendations with the MoH and the CabMin proposed committee.
- Provide briefing materials and regular opportunities for policy dialogue for new ministers, senior MoH and MoF officials who have new responsibilities in health financing policy and NHSU governance, and members of the PCC to enhance understanding of their respective roles and responsibilities.
- Implement a medium-term process for planning, priority setting, and budgeting the PMG to complement and guide the current annual process.
- Develop and implement a systematic, evidence-based methodology for defining the PMG and AMP priorities, benefit package, and tariff, together with a clear delineation of the roles of the NHSU, MoH, and MoF at each stage of development and approval.
- Develop and improve the contract specification for various services to improve quality and efficiency of services; clarify the roles of the NHSU and other parties in the process.
- Develop a framework to govern consultations over the PMG, AMP, and contract specifications that prevents conflicts of interest, promotes transparency, and ensures participation of all stakeholders, including citizens.

Long term

- Provide regular training opportunities in health financing and purchasing for the MoH and MoF staff who work with the NHSU.

- Establish formal mechanisms for NHSU subnational offices to coordinate with SNGs and hospital districts to align the NHSU's local purchasing and contracting plans with the SNG budget planning, investment planning, and transitional support for the health facilities network.
- Increase NHSU staff numbers (within the total limit already approved, but with the flexibility to reallocate posts between central and subnational offices) and develop analytical skills among NHSU staff to support the development of strategic purchasing; in the short term, the NHSU should expand and develop its subnational offices to strengthen contract monitoring and fraud control through in-person monitoring visits and performance monitoring, as a follow-up to automated monitoring.
- Develop the NHSU's IT systems to support strategic purchasing and design them to integrate with the e-Health systems to be implemented by health care providers.

NOTE

1. The NHSU includes five subnational branches: North, covering four oblasts; West, covering eight oblasts; Center, covering four oblasts; East, covering five oblasts (including Eastern Conflict Areas); and South, covering three oblasts.

REFERENCE

Maynzyuk, K. and Dzhygyr, Y. 2016. *Single National Purchaser of Health Services: Options for Organisation, Management and Financing.* Kyiv: Ministry of Health of Ukraine.